D1483781

RICH KIDS

RICH KIDS

How to Raise Our Children to Be
Happy and Successful in Life

TOM CORLEY

TWO HARBORS PRESS
MINNEAPOLIS, MN

Copyright © 2014 by Tom Corley

Two Harbors Press
322 First Avenue N, 5th floor
Minneapolis, MN 55401
612.455.2293
www.TwoHarborsPress.com

All rights reserved. No part of this publication
may be reproduced, stored in a retrieval system, or
transmitted, in any form or by any means, electronic,
mechanical, photocopying, recording, or otherwise,
without the prior written permission of the author.

ISBN-13: 978-1-62652-986-1
LCCN: 2014912429

Distributed by Itasca Books

Cover Design by Holly@BeeHavenMedia.com
Typeset by Biz Cook

Printed in the United States of America

"Every parent and child should own a copy of Rich Kids. Tom shares fantastic lessons beautifully disguised within a story!"

- *J. Money, RockstarFinance.com*

"Rich Kids is a perfect guide to assist parents in mentoring their children for success in life. Tom Corley has created a template for parent-mentoring that will enable children to reach their full potential. I strongly recommend this easy-to-read, but highly valuable book to anyone who is raising kids and want them to become way more than the average person."

Christina Skytt, International Bestselling Author of Power Goals: 9 Steps To Achieve Life-changing Goals

"Rich Kids: How to Raise Our Children to be Happy & Successful in Life contains many lessons for families trying to build a strong financial future. Although the story is targeted toward teens and young adults, the practical advice will benefit people of all ages. Tom Corley, author of Rich Habits: The Daily Success Habits of Wealthy Individuals describes specific actions people should take to ensure they will enjoy financial stability, good health and happiness. The tale is told through the eyes of a teenager who is sent to spend a summer with his wealthy and famous grandfather. Although he resents it at first and feels he is being punished by his parents, he comes to realize that the life lessons he learned that summer were an act of love and a way to prepare him for the rest of his life. Rich Kids is a guide that everyone should read, especially parents, grandparents and young adults. Implementing its practical advice will surely lead to financial freedom, good health and much happiness. I have given a copy of Rich Kids to my two young adult children. The lessons contained in the book are priceless."

Mike Kahrer, Human Resources Executive and Parent

"We were poor and my mother passed on to me some very poor habits. My Mom simply did not know any better. Rich Kids will help parents mentor their children for success and let their children know that life has no limits and that they can be, do and have anything they are willing to work for."

Marshall James, Captain, United States Army

"I read Rich Kids and loved it! I would recommend this book to all parents to read as a guideline to help their children grow up with respect and an understanding of their financial responsibilities to themselves."

Joann Zapata, Parent

"If you were looking for a manual on mentoring your child for success, this book is it."

Joe Galuski, Radio Host WSRY Syracuse

DEDICATION

This book is dedicated to the most important people in my life: my wife, Denise, and my three children, Brendan, Kirsten, and Casey. They are my *why*. They are the reason I get up at 4 a.m. and work so hard. Their pictures are plastered about the walls of my home office, where I do most of my writing and research. Those pictures inspire me every morning and every night to keep writing, no matter how tired I might be. They see me following my main purpose in life, my dream. They have witnessed my transformation from an ordinary CPA to a bestselling author. There is, in that, an important lesson in life: To follow your dreams, no matter how unrealistic they may be.

CONTENTS

ACKNOWLEDGMENTS

I am very grateful to my publicist, Lauri Flaquer. At a time when I was on the verge of quitting, Lauri entered my life, lifted me up, and inspired me. In one year's short time Lauri took an unknown, first-time, self-published author to #1 on Amazon for eight straight days. Lauri has transformed this ordinary CPA into a bestselling author. I would not be writing these words today if it were not for Lauri Flaquer. Thank you, Lauri.

I'd like to thank a few very important members of the media who put me and my rich habits research on the map. Farnoosh Torabi, from Yahoo Finance's award winning show, *Financially Fit*, was the first brave soul in the media to take a risk on this previously unknown author. Our interview went viral with over two million hits, which got the attention of Dave Ramsey. Dave Ramsey has one of the largest radio shows in the United States. My interview with Dave, together with the Yahoo interview, propelled my first book, *Rich Habits: The Daily Success Habits of Wealthy Individuals*, to #1 on Amazon for eight straight days in July 2013. Dave's continued support and promotion of my research helped keep *Rich Habits* in the top 100 of books on Amazon for much of 2013. My interview with Bob Dumas of CBS-Boston (WBZ-TV) in November of 2013 was picked up by seven CBS affiliates, which ran our interview during their nightly news segment. It was my first national television network interview and helped me gain enormous credibility with the media. Gerri Detweiler's (Credit.com) interview with me was picked up by MSN Money. The interview drew so much attention that MSN moved it to the front page from the back page and kept *Rich Habits* in the top 100 on Amazon for twenty-five straight days. Thank you all for being media leaders and taking a leap of faith with me.

I want to thank Patty Aubrey for giving me the idea to write *Rich Kids*. I met Patty in August 2013 at a Breakthrough to Success (BTS) week-long training program offered by The Canfield Training Group. I am grateful to Patty for her sage advice. Thank you, Patty.

To all the members of BTS who agreed to participate in providing feedback for this manuscript, I say thank you. Eric Whitmoyer, Aynne Johnston, Starr Pilmore, and many others from BTS all helped make *Rich Kids* a better book. I'd like to particularly thank Starr for helping me see myself as a successful author. Starr's book, *Fun with Visualization*, and her thirty-day visualization training program helped reprogram my thinking from negative to positive and enabled me to visualize myself as a bestselling author, at a time when book sales were nonexistent. Starr has helped turn my vision into a reality.

To my friend Mike Kahrer, who would sarcastically introduce me as "the famous author Tom Corley" to hostesses, bartenders, waitresses, and any other unfortunate soul who wandered into our entertainment orbit, I say thank you. Mike was instrumental in providing feedback on *Rich Kids*. He has also been one of my biggest Facebook cheerleaders, and I appreciate it.

I wish to thank all of my staff at Cerefice and Company, who work tirelessly and enthusiastically, enabling me to devote time to my writing. Without their client support efforts I would not have been able to pursue this rewarding writing career. I would like to particularly thank Mina Patel, whose work ethic, expertise, and conscientiousness are indispensable to the success of the firm.

I would like to thank Mill City Press, my publisher. Mill City's quality-consciousness and responsiveness continuously exceed my lofty expectations. I look forward to a long and mutually prosperous business relationship for many years to come.

Finally, I want to thank all of my readers. Without you, this book would not have the power to change lives. It is my mission in life to help people recognize the importance of changing their habits in order to live the life they were intended to live—a happy and successful life.

INTRODUCTION

Human beings are amazing. We are the only species on earth with the capacity to turn thoughts into reality. We all dream. We dream amazing dreams. We create amazing things from those dreams. We make the impossible possible from those dreams. And here's the thing: all of us are endowed with this innate genetic ability to create something out of nothing. There is no limit to our capacity to create, except our imagination and any limiting beliefs that hold us back in life. It was not intended for humans to be poor, to struggle financially, or to live unhappy lives. We exist to be great and to achieve great things. It is within our genetic makeup to create, to produce, to innovate, and to learn from our mistakes. We were intended to have lives of abundance, to be happy and successful.

But happiness and success do not just happen. They require the assistance of others. They require mentors. Having a mentor in life is what separates the successful from everyone else. Parents are critical to the success and happiness of children. Parents who teach their children success strategies set up their children to be happy and successful in life. Good, mentoring parents contribute to the overall betterment of society when they teach their children success strategies. Their children take these strategies with them into their adult lives. As a result, they have fulfilling careers that reward them emotionally and financially. It becomes a generational cycle of success, as our children then pass along these same success strategies to their children.

Rich Kids will help children reach their full potential. It will help them find happiness and success in life. The success strategies covered in this book are based upon my five-year study on the daily habits of successful people. In my bestselling book, *Rich Habits: The Daily Success Habits of Wealthy Individuals*, I covered the ten keystone habits that contribute to success. This book will take my research findings to the next level and share with the reader the little-known strategies successful people learned from their parents. These success strategies are unique. You won't find them anywhere else. This is because the research exposing these success strategies has never been done before. It is truly a revolutionary book.

My main purpose in writing *Rich Kids* is to help parents and grandparents mentor their children and grandchildren for success. The strategies covered will provide every parent and grandparent with a template for raising happy and successful children and grandchildren. Parents and grandparents are given a precious gift in life. They are often the only shot children have at having a mentor in life. This book will make you better parents and grandparents. It will turn you into success mentors. It will arm you with knowledge that, until now, only the wealthiest, most successful parents and grandparents, in the highest levels of society, were privy to. It will help you elevate your children to levels of success you only dreamed of.

While I wrote this book for every parent and grandparent who wants to see their children and grandchildren succeed and be happy, I also wrote *Rich Kids* to help every teacher who wants to unleash the unlimited potential of every one of their students. *Rich Kids* will open your eyes and transform you from ordinary parents, grandparents, and teachers into extraordinary mentors to the next generation.

CHAPTER ONE
THE NOTEBOOK

My oldest, Brendan, and I were embarking on our first trip together to the most sacred of places. A place where legends are made and where miracles happen. We were on our way to South Bend, Indiana, to see Notre Dame play Michigan State early in their 2014 season. It would be a long pilgrimage to South Bend: twelve hours of driving. Despite the long drive, we were both looking forward to being together to watch our favorite college football team.

Brendan is a sportsaholic. He lives and breathes just about every sport. Brendan concentrates his efforts on playing tennis, basketball, and baseball, with some intramural football and soccer thrown in, so long as it doesn't interfere. Brendan is also obsessed with Notre Dame. Part of it was my own doing. Notre Dame football is a staple in our house during football season. I also introduced Brendan to my favorite movie, *Rudy*, when he was in the fifth or sixth grade. *Rudy* is a movie about a high school student who dreams about going to Notre Dame to play football. It is a story of the classic underdog who persists and overcomes every obstacle to see his dream come true. Then, of course, there were the stories of my famous uncle who played basketball for Notre Dame for two years but left to follow his coach to Georgetown. Notre Dame was a very popular topic in our household, and Brendan had caught the bug. It was the only college on his list. He talked about going to Notre Dame practically every day. There was only one problem, his grades. Brendan, like so many in life, is a classic underachiever in school, content with getting mostly Bs, with the occasional A when the spirit moved him for whatever reason. His teachers would tell us how smart he was at every parent-teacher meeting. One teacher was so convinced of this that he talked us into having Brendan take an IQ test just to prove his point. The teacher was right. Brendan's score was higher than average. When we told Brendan this he just shrugged. When we told him that only the top students get into Notre Dame, he shrugged again. Our little excursion was, in large part, intended to light an academic fire under Brendan's butt so he could realize his dream of going to Notre Dame. Brendan had just started high school, and I thought if he saw the Notre Dame campus, the stadium, the golden dome, and Touchdown Jesus he would shift his focus more to his studies.

Not long into our journey, Brendan miraculously peeled his eyes away from his phone, looked up, and asked me about my notebook. I had carried around that notebook since I was twelve years old. I took it everywhere with me. It never left my side.

"I've been going through your notebook, Dad, when you go for your morning runs," Brendan confessed.

I was a little taken aback. I wasn't so much upset at having my personal privacy violated as I was shocked that a fourteen-year-old would actually relinquish his obsessive attachment to his phone for an old, tattered notebook.

"Why?" I asked.

He turned his head and looked out the car window as if he were searching for something in the distance. "You never talk about the notebook, but it's obviously something that's important to you. You take it just about everywhere with you. We all talk about it."

"Who's 'we'?" I asked.

"Mom, Kirsten, and Casey. We ask Mom all the time about it. She says she never read it but it has something to do with J.C."

J.C. was the name everyone in the family called Great-Grandpa Jobs.

"She said I should just ask you about it. I couldn't take it anymore, so I snuck into your briefcase and pulled it out one morning to see what was in it."

I adjusted my glasses, pushing them up the bridge of my nose, pondering my next thought. "Well?" I asked.

"Well what?" Brendan shot back.

"What did you find out? What . . . did . . . you . . . learn?" I dragged that last question out slowly, word by word.

"I thought it would be something special, something exciting, some big secret you were keeping from us, but it's all that same stuff you talk about every day. Nothing but that rich habits stuff. I guess I just thought there would be more to the notebook."

"Well, there is, Bren. There's a lot more to that notebook than meets the eye. There's a story behind what's in the notebook. J.C. taught me about the rich habits during that summer of 1984, when I was just twelve. That summer changed my life. It's the reason why we live on the water staring at New York City, why all you kids go to private school, why we've been to Hawaii and Disney twice, and why we're able to take this trip to Notre Dame. That summer, those rich habits, are the reason why we have the life that we have."

J. C. was a legend. Everyone in the family talked about him like he was some great American hero. To the world, he was J. C. Jobs, one of the most famous authors in history. J.C. had written over a hundred books, mostly about self-help and success. His books sold half a billion copies. He became an international figure and was the #1 self-help guru of his day. He helped tens of millions become incredibly successful and wealthy with his books and his teachings. He helped reduce poverty around the world and inspired a generation of millionaires. Universities named buildings after him. His Rich Habits Foundation, to this day, continues to teach the rich habits to students and the poor in over thirty countries. To our family, he was revered like a god.

"That stuff, as you call it, represents the life work of J.C. But to me it represents the most amazing summer in my life. Would you like to hear about it? It's kind of long, though."

"We've got twelve hours, Dad."

"Twelve hours? You think you can keep your eyes off your phone for that long?" I smirked.

"What phone?" Brendan smirked back, as he hit the off switch.

"OK. It was a long time ago, but I remember it like it was yesterday . . ."

CHAPTER TWO

MY SUMMER AT THE JERSEY SHORE

J.C. lived alone in a magnificent Victorian house, a block from Manasquan Beach, at the Jersey Shore. My own dad told me that Grandma Jobs had died when they were very young and J.C. raised them himself, as a single parent. He never remarried. He said J.C. was so in love with Grandma that he could never bring himself to love another woman. J.C. used to be a CPA but wrote a book called *Rich Habits* that became an international bestseller that, overnight, turned him into a household name. He moved the family down the shore soon after, and my dad and his two sisters grew up at the Jersey Shore. Over the years, J.C. revamped the house into a much larger six-bedroom Victorian with a huge wraparound porch. Three of the rooms had dual bunk beds. Each bunk bed could sleep three kids. Oftentimes, the house would be packed with six cousins bunking together in each room. We spent a lot of time at that shore house. Every Easter, Thanksgiving, Christmas, and summer my two sisters and I and all the cousins would get together with J.C. at the shore house. We all thought of it as our shore house. That's the way J.C. liked it. Surrounded by his family.

Summers were filled with barbecues, golf outings, and parties on every holiday weekend. It was heaven on earth. J.C.

built a barn-size Irish pub in the backyard. He stocked the bar in his Irish pub with every type of beer known to man. J.C. loved his beer, but I never, ever saw him drunk. He used to say all the time, "everything in moderation." The main floor of the pub had a long bar with one of those authentic Skee-Ball tables off to the side. One section of the bar had all sorts of electronic games. My favorites were Pac-Man and Asteroids. Another section had a huge fireplace encircled by the largest sectional couch you ever saw. The bar even had a section dedicated just to darts. It had a basement, with a custom-built, walk-in humidor that went from one side of the basement to the other. J.C. loved his cigars, too. On the top floor of the pub was J.C.'s office. When the family wasn't around, J.C. would practically live in that office. He was always working on another book, or preparing for another lecture or some training gig. He never stopped teaching the rich habits. The family would tell him he worked too hard, but J.C. used to say that "passion knows no time clock." J.C. lived and breathed those rich habits.

I remember I had just come home from school. It was 1984 and I was wrapping up the seventh grade. I was looking forward to summer. I had just taken off my school uniform and was sitting at my desk when my mom walked into my room. She told me that she and Dad had given it a lot of thought and decided I would be spending the entire summer with J.C. at the shore house. I remember nearly falling off my chair in shock. I immediately told her there was no way I was going to spend my summer with J.C. away from all my friends. I loved J.C. but he was my sixty-eight-year-old grandpa. I didn't want to spend my summer with my grandpa. I got so emotional I started crying. But Mom wouldn't budge. When my dad came home I practically launched myself at him as he was walking through the door, pleading with him to let me stay home. Another argument broke out, more yelling and tears. But he and my mom were a united front. I was going to spend the summer with J.C. and that was that. I stomped up to my room, slammed the door as hard as I could, collapsed on my bed, and buried my face into the pillow. After a few minutes, my dad opened the door to my room and sat down at the side of my bed. He patted me on the back and told me that a lot of thought and planning had gone into this summer. Dad said, "There was a purpose behind our decision."

Hoping it would ease the pain, my dad told me that J.C. said it was OK if my friends visited and stayed over every now and then. I kept my head buried in the pillow, even after my dad made his way out of my room. I kept asking myself what I did wrong. Why were they punishing me? I wanted to run away from home. I actually thought about running away from home that night.

The day I arrived at the shore house, J.C. greeted me with a notebook and a mechanical pencil.

"What's this?" I asked.

"You're gonna need it. Every day," was all J.C. said.

I had no idea what J.C. had in store for me that summer or how that notebook would shape the rest of my life.

CHAPTER THREE

THE THREE PATHS TO WEALTH

I was still fast asleep when J.C. woke me that first morning. It was early, much earlier than I was used to waking up for school.

"Come on! Up and at 'em!" J.C. barked.

I rubbed my eyes and saw J.C. standing at the foot of my bed in his jogging outfit, ready for action. J.C. had these outrageous neon yellow Converse sneakers on that screamed at my morning eyes. It was all I could do to avert them from the painful glow.

J.C. was tall, around six four, thin, yet muscular. I never thought of him as old, like grandfathers were supposed to be, because he looked so young and was always in motion. My mom used to tell my sisters and me that J.C. exercised every day and watched what he ate. He had one of those military haircuts. I always assumed he was a former marine, but my mom just said he liked his hair that way.

As I crawled out of bed, stretched, and rubbed my eyes, I thought to myself that this was going to be the summer from hell.

"Brush your teeth and be down in fifteen, we're headed to the boardwalk," J.C. said, walking out of the bedroom with that signature salute he gave all the grandkids. He'd raise his right hand to the side of his chin, transform it into a gun, and make this "click" sound, like he just fired the gun at us. I always found it amusing, but not that day at five in the morning. My intuition told me I was going to grow to hate that salute.

I barely stepped foot into the kitchen when J.C. said, "Get your notebook."

I slugged back upstairs and swiped it off my dresser and slugged back down to the kitchen.

"Three paths to wealth."

I looked across the kitchen table at J.C. with a blank stare.

"'Three paths to wealth,' write it down at the top of the first page," J.C. commanded.

So I pulled the pencil out from inside the twirly spine of the notebook and wrote at the top of the page "Three Paths to Wealth," just as J.C. instructed.

"Leave the notebook on the table. We'll get to that later," J.C. instructed

We strolled out the door. The house was only a block from the beach, so it didn't take long to get to the boardwalk.

"Here's the process," J.C. said as he put his hand on my shoulder.

"We walk, I talk, and you listen. When we're done walking we'll head back home and I'll fix us some breakfast and talk some more as you write. Then we'll eat and go over the lesson just to make sure you got everything right."

I was so angry with my parents. I kept thinking what a lousy summer this was going to be. I felt I was being punished by them and I had no idea why. But I was stuck now. Stuck with J.C. at the Jersey Shore for the whole summer.

J.C. and I began to walk and he began to talk.

"There are only three known ways to accumulate wealth: #1, living below your means; #2, expanding your means; or #3, following both #1 and #2.

LIVING BELOW YOUR MEANS

I like to refer to this as the 80:20 rule. It's a simple rule really, and I consider it a Rich Habit. This rule requires that you set aside 20 percent of every paycheck and learn to live off the remaining 80 percent. You do this no matter how much money you make. If you get a raise or bonus, set aside 20 percent of that raise or bonus, in addition to the 20 percent on your regular pay. If you stick to the 80:20 rule you will save a lot of money and you'll be wealthy long before you reach retirement age. You will be one of the few wealthy ones among your friends and colleagues because, unfortunately, most parents don't teach their kids the importance of saving, so nobody saves.

When it comes to spending that 80 percent, here's some advice. It'll come in handy when you're a little older:

- **Don't spend more than 25 percent of your monthly net pay on housing. It doesn't matter if you own or rent. Stick to this 25 percent rule.**

- **Don't spend more than 10 percent of your monthly net pay on entertainment. This includes movies, restaurants, bars, etc.**

- **Don't spend more than 5 percent of your monthly net pay on auto loans, and never lease. Leasing is a poverty habit. Buy your cars and take good care of them.**

- Stay away from accumulating credit card debt. If you are doing this, it means you are living beyond your means and you need to cut back on something.

- Always invest your savings prudently. Never gamble your savings on get-rich-quick schemes. There's no such thing. The power of compounding interest can grow your savings and make you wealthy.

- When you start working, max out your contributions to the company pension plan, if they allow it.

- Know what you spend every month. Create a monthly budget and track what you spend."

J.C. paused. He seemed to be trying to gather his thoughts. I was amazed that all this stuff was effortlessly flowing straight out of his head. No notes, no book, no recording devices, and no index cards. Just plain old memory. After a minute or so he continued.

"Most of the wealthy don't make a lot of money. But they do save a lot. They make a habit of saving until it hurts. They focus on accumulating wealth through savings. Savings and investments are two different things. Your savings should never lose money, whereas your investments represent a portion of your savings that you are willing to put at risk and potentially lose. How much you take out of your savings and invest depends on your risk tolerance. Conservative wealthy people do not put any of their savings at risk. Moderate wealthy people put 25 to 50 percent of their savings at risk. Aggressive wealthy people put 50 percent or more of their savings at risk.

"If the wealthy invest part of their savings, they typically invest it in one or more of the following:

- **Their businesses.**
- **Their pensions.**
- **Guaranteed products like life insurance.**
- **Stocks and bonds.**
- **Real estate investments.**
- **Gold.**
- **Education for their children.**

Accumulating wealth is not about hitting it out of the baseball park. It's about getting singles. You get enough singles and you win the game.

EXPANDING YOUR MEANS

This path often involves taking on some risk. It may require investing some of your savings. The risk is often both in time and money. But expanding your means does not always involve significant financial risk. You could expand your means by starting a part-time business, getting involved in multilevel marketing, creating something that you could sell at a flea market, or developing a new skill that could eventually help you make more money. These things do take time, but that's the point, isn't it? You're using your time productively. It's an investment in yourself. You're young. Now's the best time to start developing skills that you could one day use to make money. Time is definitely on your side when you're young. Learn as many new skills as you can when you're young. They'll come in handy when you're older and need to make more money in life. You'll have something to fall back on when you need it the most.

APPLYING BOTH STRATEGIES

If you apply both the 80:20 rule and the "expand your means" strategy, you'll get rich faster. Expanding your means and the 80:20 rule are powerful strategies used by many of the most successful individuals to accumulate wealth, which allows them to retire without any financial worries."

We finished our walk, found a bench, and sat down and watched the waves crash against the sand. J.C. shifted his glance from the waves and then back to me.

"Look, I know you must be asking yourself, 'What the hell have I gotten myself into? What did I do wrong?' Here's the thing, though: I love you. Your parents love you. This is what I do for a living. People pay thousands and thousands of dollars to have me speak. They don't pay me all that money for my looks. I know how to take someone, anyone, and make them rich. I don't care if you're dirt poor, have one parent, no parents, no job. I don't care if they're straight out of jail or even have some physical disability. It doesn't matter."

J.C. turned his gaze back to the ocean. "The things I'm going to teach you this summer are going to change your life. What I'm going to teach you will put you far ahead of the competition in life. Very few parents teach their kids the things I'm going to teach you this summer. You could spend the next twenty years in school and never learn the most important things a person needs to learn in life: how to get rich and how to be happy. You can thank me later."

I didn't much care about money. I was twelve at the time. What I cared about was playing tennis, basketball, and baseball and watching other people do those things. I was so pissed off at my parents after that first walk with J.C. I was absolutely convinced that that summer was going to be the worst summer a kid could have.

J.C. did just as he said. He cooked breakfast, he talked, and I wrote. He repeated everything he said on the boardwalk about the three paths to wealth. I don't think he changed a word. It was like listening to a recording. I was amazed at that.

When we finished breakfast, J.C. pulled his chair next to mine and reviewed my notes. When he found something that I had written down that was wrong, he had me erase it and then correct it. I realized then why J.C. gave me a mechanical pencil. Man, he just did not miss a beat. We spent a lot of time correcting my notes until J.C. was satisfied.

That's pretty much how our morning lessons went that summer. A lot of teaching, writing, and correcting. All before most people were even getting up to start their day.

"Tired?" J.C. asked after we'd made all our corrections.

"A little," I said.

"OK. I'm going to head into my office. You take a nap and in a few hours we'll get going."

Oh crap, I moaned inside my head. Going where? How much worse can this get? I wondered.

After a couple of hours of some much needed rest, J.C. was back in my room waking me up again.

"Did your mom pack your tennis stuff?" he asked.

"Yeah," I shot back, still groggy and grouchy from being woken up.

"Good. Let's hit the tennis courts."

I had no desire to play tennis with J.C. Christ, he was my grandpa. I didn't care how fit he was, he was still sixty-eight and I was one of the best tennis players in my age bracket back home. I had no desire to watch a sixty-eight-year-old try to return my shots. I decided it was time for retribution. I was going to take out my revenge for this summer on the tennis courts with J.C. When I was done with J.C. he'd never ask me to play tennis again, I thought to myself. I was going to punish him.

When we got to the courts, J.C. opened the back door of his station wagon. It was filled with all sorts of sports equipment. Baseballs, bats, basketballs, and tennis gear. He pulled out a large yellow basket filled with tennis balls and this huge bag filled with his tennis rackets. I'd only ever seen a bag that big on TV when I watched the tennis pros walk onto the court.

J.C. had us do some stretches and a few side to side shuffles. Then he brought his basket of balls to the middle of the baseline, on his side of the court, and told me we were going to run some drills. For the next hour J.C. drilled me on backhands, forehands, volleys, overheads, and serves.

When we were done he challenged me to a set. Here we go, I thought to myself. Here comes the beat down.

J.C. proceeded to annihilate me. I didn't get a game. Worse, I couldn't return any of his serves. They came at me too fast or with too much spin. His second serve had so much topspin on it that it bounced way over my head, out of my reach. He cleaned my clock 6-0 in about twenty minutes. I was in a state of complete shock.

"By the end of the summer you'll not only be returning my serves, you'll be beating me," J.C. said as we packed away the tennis gear.

I felt humiliated, and J.C. must have sensed this.

"Look, I've been playing tennis since I was nine. It was one of my obsessions in life. At seventeen I was ranked in the top ten in the Northeast in the eighteen and under division. I was a teaching pro in high school and college. Don't feel so bad. Sports is in our genes. Your great-grandfather was drafted by the St. Louis Cardinals. Your great-uncle is in the hall of fame at Georgetown University for basketball and played nine years in the pros. You're hardwired for success. It's in your genes. It's in everyone's genes. All humans are hardwired for success. We all have what I like to call the genius gene. We just have to learn to activate it. But we'll talk about that tomorrow."

When we reached the car, J.C. popped the trunk and dumped all the tennis gear in the back, then shut the trunk and turned to me. "Feel like playing some b-ball?" he smirked.

We finally got back to the house around 2 p.m. Four hours of tennis, basketball, and baseball with J.C. I was exhausted. I couldn't believe the shape he was in. I must have shot about two hundred free throws with J.C., pitched a hundred pitches to him, and batted hundreds of balls, all thrown by J.C. It felt like I was at sports camp.

When we got home, J.C. threw some burgers on the grill and set the picnic table outside.

"Think you can handle me?" J.C. said, as I wolfed down my burger.

"It won't be so bad," he said before I could muster up a response.

"Here's the plan. One week on, one week off," J.C. boomed. He then proceeded to explain our summer schedule.

"One week of work and one week of fun. On the off weeks you can have your friends sleep over. Have as many as you like. One, ten, twenty. I don't care. Just let me know. Work hard, play hard. You've got to learn to reward yourself after working hard. But that's a lesson for another day."

J.C. paused, to give me time to digest the summer schedule.

"Get in touch with your friends. See who wants to sleep over next week. Let me know how many."

No way, I thought to myself. I'm not dragging them into this camp of J.C.'s. J.C. was reading my thoughts.

"Look, I've got a lot of fun things planned for next week. We're gonna hit Shea Stadium and see the Mets play, then we're gonna take the RV and camp out for a night, then the amusement park in Ocean City. Got it all figured out. No lessons next week, just fun."

When I finished my lunch, I ran to the kitchen phone and immediately called my friends.

So, that's how the summer went. One week of J.C.'s camp and one week of play. Those off weeks were incredible. J.C. was true to his word. On the weekends Mom and Dad would visit. I was really happy to see them. It was like a family reunion every weekend.

CHAPTER FOUR

THE GENIUS GENE

Day two started out exactly like day one. I brought my notebook down to the kitchen table and stared at J.C. as he sipped his coffee.

"Today we're going to talk about the 'genius' gene."

I opened my notebook, took out my pencil, and wrote across the top of the page: 'The Genius Gene.'

The lesson began as soon as we got out the front door.

"Human beings are the only species on earth who have the ability to convert thought into substance. We think intangible things and we create tangible works of art. The Brooklyn Bridge, the Eiffel Tower, and the Sears Tower."

I honestly had no idea what or where the Sears Tower was and, once again, I sensed J.C. crawling inside my head.

"The Sears Tower is located in Chicago. It is the tallest building in the world at 1,450 feet. Its height almost reaches the cloud barrier. Towards heaven." J.C. paused and looked over to me.

"What's your limit?" It must have been a rhetorical question, because J.C. didn't wait for my response.

"None. Human beings are the most amazing species to inhabit the earth. We are in many respects all geniuses." J.C. paused again to let it sink in, then continued the lesson.

"A lot of books have been written about God. The most famous one is the Bible. Whenever you read about God, at the core of being God is one unique trait: the ability to create. This ability makes God unique. But God is not the only one who can create. Humans also possess this trait. We are the only species on earth who have the innate ability to create tangible things from mere thought. We have the ability to dream and turn those dreams into reality. Each of us is endowed with the genius gene. Those who create are actually tapping into the genius gene. Those individuals who turn on this genius gene and create things of value to society are labeled 'geniuses' and rewarded by society. They can make a lot of money and become famous for their creations. Only when we create are we truly being human. For some unknown reason, we are the only species on earth blessed with this unique gift to turn thoughts into reality. Those who spend their lives creating are the happiest and most fulfilled of all human beings. Happiness is life's main reward for utilizing the genius gene. Creating is our purpose in life. For most, unfortunately, it remains dormant. When we fail to use our genius gene, we never learn what our main purpose in life is. We become lost. So many are lost." J.C. drifted off for a moment, lost in thought. He had a sad expression on his face for a moment and then resumed the lesson.

"When you don't activate your genius gene, you find yourself unhappy, eking out a living, and you never reach your full potential in life. Making use of the genius gene is the path to happiness, success, and wealth. Ignoring it is the path to misery, failure, and poverty.

ACTIVATING THE GENIUS GENE

If you want to be truly happy in life you must activate the genius gene. You do this by engaging in some creative activity. Creativity comes in many forms. Some people, like myself, activate their genius gene by writing, some through music, others by teaching, painting, building something, manufacturing something, inventing something, athletics, acting, etc. The key is to be able to engage in some lifelong creative activity that also pays you enough money to help support a family. If you can make money engaging in a creative activity you will never work a day in your life. At least it won't feel like work. And you'll want to engage in that creative activity all the time, even on weekends.

You can't be successful in life if you don't have a passion for what you do for a living, and you can only find your passion in life by pursuing creative activities. When you engage in some creative activity, you activate the genius gene, which then stimulates your passion and inspires even more creative activity. No mountain stands in the way of a man with a passion. Find your passion and you can move mountains. But we'll talk more about how to do that tomorrow."

CHAPTER FIVE

FINDING YOUR MAIN PURPOSE IN LIFE

When I woke, it was pouring rain outside. I was sure that meant no lesson that day, but just then J.C. burst into my room. "Gonna rain all day. No worries, we're headed to the gym."

J.C. had this awesome gym above his garage. It had all sorts of exercise equipment. Treadmills, something called a StairMaster, stationary bikes, and free weights. You name it, he had it. There were these huge twenty inch TV screens scattered here and there, mounted on the walls. J.C.'s StairMaster, treadmills, and stationary bikes all had this makeshift device that held his books. He said he did a lot of his reading on those machines.

"I just love reading my books while I'm working out," he said. "I like to highlight things in them and make notes in the margins."

J.C. jumped on his StairMaster and pointed me to a nearby treadmill and we began the lesson for the day.

"Happiness is elusive. Most people are, in fact, unhappy. There was a famous writer named Henry David Thoreau who said: 'Most men lead lives of quiet desperation . . .' Most people are unhappy because they are struggling financially. They are struggling financially because either they are living beyond their means or their job simply does not provide them with a sufficient income. Odds are, when you are not making a sufficient income at your job, it's because you're doing something you don't particularly like. When you can earn a sufficient income doing something you enjoy, that's when you know you've found your main purpose in life.

But how do you find your main purpose in life? Believe it or not, finding your main purpose in life is completely within your control. Here's the process: Make a list of everything you can remember that made you happy in life. Hopefully, it's a long list. Now highlight those items on your list which involve a skill. Next assign a job-type designation to each of the highlighted items. Then rank each of the highlighted items in terms of happiness, with #1 being the greatest happiness and #2 the next greatest happiness and so on. Now rank each of the highlighted items in terms of income potential, with #1 being the highest income and #2 being the next highest and so on. Last thing you do is total the two columns. The lowest scores represent your main purpose in life."

After breakfast J.C. and I went over the notes and he helped me devise the following chart:

MAIN PURPOSE

DESCRIPTION	JOB CATEGORIES	HAPPY	$	TOTAL
When I ran the campaign for class President	Politician, Campaign Manager, Professional Speaker	1	3	4
When I organized the ski trip for our high school class	Event Planning	2	2	4
When I coached basketball in college	Basketball Coach	3	4	7
When I worked part-time in college selling cars	New Car Salesman, New Car Dealership Owner	6	1	7
When I wrote for the school newspaper	Journalist, Author	4	5	9
When I was part of ROTC in high school	Military Career	5	6	11

We went indoors for sports camp that day. J.C. liked to mix up the routine every now and then. Some days we played every sport, others just one. That day was one of those days. Nothing but baseball. We went to a local indoor baseball facility about a mile from J.C.'s house. J.C. had me bat for a while, then field grounders, and then finish off with a half hour of pitching with the facility pitching coach.

The coach used to pitch for the Phillies in his younger days and now trained kids how to pitch. J.C. said three of the coach's "kids" were now playing in the majors, so he was kind of famous. He showed me how to throw a curve, screw ball, slider, and rising fastball, and how to place the pitch inside, outside, high, and low. He said the best pitchers were the ones who pitched the longest in the majors. He said they all had one thing in common. They all had command of their pitches. Control was the key. So that summer I learned how to pitch with control.

CHAPTER SIX

THE SUCCESS SEESAW

The rain subsided and it was back to the boardwalk for another morning lesson.

"Today we're going to learn about the 'success seesaw' and how to get your seesaw tipping in the right direction."

And, with that, the lesson began.

"Forty percent of all of our daily activities are habits. This means 40 percent of the time we are all on auto pilot. Forty percent of the time we don't even think about what we are doing during the day. We are all in zombie mode 40 percent of the time. Now, if you have good daily habits, then this is a good thing. But if you have bad daily habits, then this is a bad thing. Without much thought, we are all either on the path to creating wealth or on the path to creating poverty. Daily habits are responsible for our wealth, poverty, happiness, and unhappiness," J.C. said, and then continued the lesson.

"Our daily habits come primarily from our parents. If your parents raise you with good daily habits, then you will very likely grow up to be wealthy and happy. If your parents raise you with bad daily habits, then you will very likely grow up poor and unhappy. This is the true cause of the wealth gap, and it's the reason the rich get richer and the poor get poorer.

Habits are stored in our basal ganglia, which is smack in the middle of the brain. The brain intentionally isolates our habits away from the rest of the brain. This allows the brain to function more efficiently, since very little brain processing power is required to initiate a habit. This is intended to be a good thing, as it frees up the brain for other important functions. If you have good habits, this is a very good thing, because without much thought, you are moving toward success. However, if you have bad habits, this is a bad thing, because without much thought you are moving towards poverty and failure in life. The good news is that habits can be changed.

Now visualize a seesaw. Imagine on one side of your seesaw are all of your good habits and on the other side are all of your bad habits. From here on I'll be referring to good habits as rich habits and bad habits as poverty habits.

Those who are wealthy and successful in life have far more rich habits than they have poverty habits. Those who are poor and struggling financially have far more poverty habits than rich habits. Those stuck in the middle are called the middle class. The middle class have about an equal number of rich habits and poverty habits. Getting your seesaw to tip in the right direction may be as simple as changing just a few daily habits. For example, if you are in the middle class and you want to become wealthy, you only have to add a few rich habits or eliminate a few poverty habits. If you are poor and you want to become wealthy, you'll have to add three or four rich habits or eliminate as many poverty habits.

The point I'm making here is that the difference between being poor or middle class is only a few habits, requiring only a few minor changes to your daily routine. I put together a chart for you that will help you understand what I'm talking about here."

After breakfast we reviewed my notes and J.C. and I also went over a copy of J.C.'s Rich Habits vs. Poverty Habits chart. J.C. opened a small desk drawer just off the kitchen and pulled out some tape.

"Here, tape that chart right here."

So I taped the chart you're looking at to my notebook.

ACTIVITY	RICH HABIT	POVERTY HABIT
Communication	I am very careful what I say and how I say it	I believe in saying what's on my mind
Daily Goals	I maintain a To-Do list every day	I do not maintain a To-Do list every day
Delayed Gratification	I believe in planning for tomorrow	I believe in living for today
Eating	I watch what I eat every day. I eat less than 300 junk food calories each day	I eat what I want when I want, including junk food
Eating	I count my calories and watch what I eat every day	I never count calories
Exercise	I exercise aerobically 30 minutes or more, four days a week	I do not exercise aerobically on a regular basis
Fate	I do not believe in fate	I believe in fate
Gamble	I rarely gamble	I like to gamble or play the lottery regularly
Goals	I achieve most of my goals in life	I don't set goals
Goals	All of my goals are in writing and I constantly review them	I do not have any goals
Luck	I am lucky	I am not lucky. In fact I'm unlucky
Morning Routine	I wake up 3 hours prior to arriving at work. I spend my time reading, exercising or doing other things to further my career or knowledge	I wake up, shower and commute to work
Networking	I network 5 hours or more each month	I don't like to network and avoid it
Parenting	I teach my children good daily success habits	I never learned good daily success habits from my parents. I'm not sure what success habits I should be teaching my children
Parenting	I make my children volunteer 10 hours or more each month	I do not make my children volunteer
Parenting	I make my children read 2 or more educational or self-improvement books each month	I do not make my children read for self-improvement
Reading	I read 2 educational or career-related books each month	If I read, I read books on fiction or for entertainment
Reading	I read 30 minutes or more each day of educational, self-improvement or career-related material	I do not read any educational, self-improvement or career-related books
Savings	I save 20% or more of my net paycheck and live off the remaining 80%	I cannot afford to save
T.V.	I watch less than 1 hour of T.V. each day	I watch more than 1 hour of T.V. each day
Volunteer	I volunteer 5 hours or more each month	I do not volunteer on a regular basis

Brendan and I had been driving for about three hours on our father-son journey to South Bend. I turned my head towards him and could see he had the page of my notebook opened to the "Success Seesaw" lesson and was looking at the chart. At that moment a wave of emotions enveloped me. I felt this strong surge of love pulsating through my body. I realized, then, what J.C. must have felt so many years ago while teaching me his rich habits. I felt love.

"Want to take a break from the story?" I asked Brendan.

"No way, Dad. Keep going. Keep going. I want to hear more about J.C."

So I went on with the story of my 1984 summer down the Jersey Shore with J.C.

CHAPTER SEVEN
THE AVALANCHE OF SUCCESS

J.C. started out the next day's lesson by telling me how success usually comes in downpours that follow long droughts of nothingness.

"At times, the nothingness can drag you down. Success requires patience. But then big, noticeable events occur in the lives of the successful that help transform their lives.

Success is not easy. Success takes time, persistence, passion, and an obsessiveness that borders on fanaticism. Successful people are fanatics. They are obsessed. They understand that success is a process. They do certain things every single day that set them apart from everyone else, which positions them to be financially successful. The pursuit of success is a psychological minefield. The ups and downs you experience in the pursuit of success are impossible to explain. Suffice it to say that this success process requires a dogged determination and a steel mind."

J.C. continued. "The path towards success requires that you do little things every day. Wealthy, successful people have good daily habits taught to them primarily by their parents. They incorporate these good daily habits into their everyday lives. These good daily habits are part of their toolkit for success. Most people have unintentionally learned bad habits from their parents. This is why most individuals struggle financially, eking out a living, and live paycheck to paycheck.

In my five-year research study on the good daily habits wealthy parents pass along to their children, I discovered ten habits that put you on the path towards success. These ten habits are at the heart of the success process. I call them the rich habits. When you follow these rich habits you're actually walking in the footsteps of the wealthy. You're processing success into your life.

But it takes time. Successful people understand that by following the rich habits every day, they are getting closer and closer to the 'success event,' or what I call the 'avalanche of success' event.

By doing certain things every day, by processing success into their lives through the application of the rich habits, wealthy individuals understand that they are actually positioning themselves for an avalanche of success event. Each day you follow the rich habits you get closer and closer to the avalanche of success event." J.C. paused and drew in a long breath.

"Here's how it works. You follow the rich habits every day. Over time, opportunity luck builds and builds, like snowflakes on a mountainside. These snowflakes, this opportunity luck, eventually becomes so significant that an avalanche will occur in your life. This avalanche is the byproduct of following the rich habits every day. The financial rewards always are disproportionate to the daily efforts you put out by following the rich habits, but that is the reality of wealth creation. The rewards, when they arrive, seem obscene compared to your daily efforts. The avalanche of success works. Wealthy people have been using this technique for thousands of years to create incredible wealth."

During breakfast I asked J.C. what the rich habits were. He told me that he would go into more detail about the rich habits next week. So I put my notebook away until the next lesson.

CHAPTER EIGHT

THE OFF WEEK

The first off week was a blast. True to his word, J.C. let me have some of my friends stay the week at the shore house. What a blast. One of J.C.'s friends let J.C. use his luxury box seats at Shea Stadium to watch the Mets play the Phillies.

"Shea was the old Mets stadium, right Dad?" Brendan asked.

"Right. They tore it down a few years ago and built a new stadium. It's called Citi Field now."

Brendan nodded.

None of us had ever been in a luxury box before. They had all sorts of food: hot dogs, burgers, fries, you name it. After a few innings, J.C. took us for a tour around the stadium and bought us all Mets jerseys and caps. He spent a lot of money on us that day. My friends thought J.C. was the greatest grandpa a kid could have.

The next day J.C. took us to Jenkinson's, an amusement park in Point Pleasant Beach, and we went on all the rides, got cotton candy, candy apples, played games at the arcade, and walked along the boardwalk.

On the third day it rained, so J.C. declared it 'movie day' and we went to a big movie theater and watched three movies back to back. J.C. liked comedies and science fiction, so he made a deal that he would sit through one of our movies if we sat through two of his movies.

On the fourth day J.C. took us to the water park at Great Adventure. J.C. went on all the water rides with us, including the big tube ride, where everyone sits in a big tube while it drops down three stories. It was a hot day, a perfect day to be wet.

After Great Adventure, we all piled into J.C.'s RV and headed to Big Timber Lake campgrounds in Cape May. We set up some tents and J.C. got a good fire going. We sat around under the stars and listened for hours to J.C.'s stories about all the countries he'd been to and all of the famous people he had met in life. He knew so many famous people. J.C. said many of them had been his rich habits students.

On the last day J.C. took us to the Ocean City Zoo. They had all sorts of exotic animals there: zebras, elephants, ostriches, kangaroos, huge rat-like animals that we learned were called capybaras.

That week I told my friends all about J.C.'s success camp. I showed them the notebook and even read through a few of J.C.'s lessons. They thought success camp was boring, so I changed the subject. I then told them about the afternoon sports camp. They liked the sports camp stuff. They thought it was pretty cool and wished they had a grandpa like mine. I felt something begin to stir in me after that off week. That something soon became a thought that this might not be such a bad summer after all.

CHAPTER NINE
THE THREE TRAITS OF SUCCESSFUL PEOPLE

With the first off week now just a happy memory, we went back to our routine. J.C. called today's boardwalk lesson, "The Three Traits of Successful People."

"Wealthy, successful people all share three traits: focus, persistence, and patience," J.C. said.

FOCUS

"Focus is either forced or unforced," J.C. explained.

"Forced focus is not fun. In fact, forced focus is commonly known by another name—work. Forced focus is usually driven by deadlines and job commitments.

Unforced focus is something completely different. It's not work. It's a unique type of focus that just happens. It's the most powerful type of focus because it's a more intense type of focus with a very long shelf life. Successful people have been known to focus on a goal, in pursuit of their main purpose, for years without the focus diminishing. Finding your main purpose in life results in unforced focus. When you find your main purpose in life, passion creates an incredible desire to act. It's almost beyond your control. You're helpless in its power. Here's the formula: Main Purpose = Passion = Unforced Focus.

You know you have unforced focus when all you think about is your main purpose. It fills your every waking moment. You become obsessed. Unforced focus allows you to overcome all of the roadblocks that life puts in your way. When you find your main purpose in life you stop worrying about the 'how.' The 'why' is all that matters. The 'why' is your main purpose. Once you find your 'why,' the 'how' magically appears. Life automatically shows you the way. Unforced focus allows you to become better, learn new skills, and facilitates the manifestation of the creative solutions that will overcome all obstacles that are standing between your current reality and your future reality.

PERSISTENCE

Persistence is sustained effort towards a goal or your main purpose. Most people lack persistence, and it is the reason most are not wealthy. A lack of persistence is the main cause of failure in life. Wealthy people have this rich habit of persistence. They simply never give up. They are obsessed with their goals and their main purpose.

Life is a funny thing. When we pursue our dreams, life places obstacles in our way, and we ask, why? Life makes our path seemingly impassible, and we ask, why? Life puts our backs against the wall, and we ask, why? Here's my answer to that why. Life forces all dreamers to persist. Persistence sharpens us. It enables us to overcome future obstacles more easily. Life isn't working against us—it's working for us. Every obstacle is an education. Every mistake is a learning experience. Every obstacle forces us to a higher level. It forces us to evolve. Every obstacle makes us more perfect."

J.C. gave an example.

"The Battle of Britain was the longest aerial campaign ever. The Royal Air Force relentlessly defended Britain against the German Luftwaffe. After nearly four months of this relenting defense, the Germans decided not to invade Britain and shifted their sights to Russia, thus ending the Battle of Britain and changing the outcome of the war."

PATIENCE

J.C. said patience, for him, was the hardest of the three traits.

"No matter how hard you focus and persist, success takes time. Realizing your goals in life just takes time. Life is a marathon," he said.

"You need to approach life that way. If you don't, you'll lose your patience and quit. Patience is born of faith and a never-ending belief that you will achieve your main purpose in life. Belief makes miracles happen. The obstacles life throws in your way will test your patience. Understanding that there is a good reason for those obstacles, self-improvement, makes it easier to patiently persist. Being patient tells life, 'I will persist until I achieve my goals and fulfill my main purpose.'

Success is always right around the corner. It's hiding behind a mountain of mistakes and failures. You just can't see it right away. It's shy. It wants to get to know you better. To see if you have what it takes. Success only introduces itself to you when it realizes you will not quit.

I want you to ignore those in life who tell you it can't be done. Don't listen to anyone who tells you to stop dreaming, to stop pursuing your silly dream. Ignore them when they tell you you're just not good enough or that you're not smart enough. Unfortunately, most dream killers are the very people who you love the most, the people who are closest to you. Don't let them stop you or tear you down. You are much more than you ever imagined. Be patient and persist towards your goals in life. You only find out how amazing you truly are when your back is up against the wall and your dream feels like it's collapsing under the weight of all of your failures and mistakes. When you are about ready to quit, but for some reason don't, that is when life blinks. And oh, what a blink. It is always some unintended consequence that happens. Something completely out of the blue that you never expected and could never have imagined. When you patiently persist, life bends to your will. It goes from adversary to ally."

When we finished breakfast, we walked over to J.C.'s office on top of his Irish pub. It never failed to impress me, his office. Half of his office looked like a mini library, with a dozen bookshelves lined up one after another. J.C. rarely bragged. He considered it a poverty habit. But when it came to his books he would violate his own bragging poverty habit rule, telling those closest to him that he had more books than Thomas Jefferson. I didn't know how many books Jefferson had, so I asked him. J.C. said Jefferson had over two thousand books. He sold them to the federal government and they used his books to start the Library of Congress.

J.C. handed me a list of specific books he wanted me to read that summer. He then grabbed a large tote bag, gave the bag to me, and told me to follow him. We walked to the self-help section of his personal library and J.C. began pulling books off the shelves, one after another, in the following order of priority:

1. *Rich Habits* by J.C. Jobs

2. *The Power of Your Subconscious Mind* by
    Joseph Murphy

3. *How to Win Friends and Influence People* by
    Dale Carnegie

4. *The Silva Mind Control Method for Getting
    Help From Your Other Side* by Jose Silva

5. *Think and Grow Rich* by Napoleon Hill

6. *Psycho Cybernetics* by Maxwell Maltz

7. *The Magic of Believing* by Claude Bristol

8. *The Power of Positive Thinking* by Norman
    Vincent Peale

9. *The Richest Man in Babylon* by George Clason

10. *The Strangest Secret* by Earl Nightingale

When we were done, J.C. carried the bag back to the house and up the stairs to my room. He dropped the bag of books by the desk in my room, put the list on the desk, and then sat down on my bed.

"These are now your books. I want you to read as many as you can before the summer is out."

J.C. stood up and walked over to the window and stared out of it.

"We're going to switch things up a bit," he said.

J.C. then turned and walked back to my desk, pulled *Rich Habits* from the bag, and handed it to me.

"After breakfast I want you to read this book until you're done. It should take you about three hours. After you're done, I've got another surprise for you. If you need me, I'll be in my office."

J.C. headed out the room and I plopped on my bed and read *Rich Habits*. This was the first book J.C. ever wrote. After about three hours, I finished the book and, like clockwork, I heard J.C. walking up the stairs. Before I knew it, he was standing in the doorway of my bedroom.

"You done?"

"Yep," I said. "Just finished it. How'd you know I'd be done?" I asked J.C.

"I wrote the damn book," J.C. barked. "Get your tennis gear. We're headed to the club. Be down in ten."

The pro at J.C.'s club was a former touring pro. He coached some of the best in the game. Two kids he coached were now famous tennis pros, John McEnroe and Vitas Gerulaitis. As a result, he could afford to be very selective about who he picked to coach. That summer, thanks to J.C., he picked me. The coach was one of J.C.'s many rich habits disciples. He was also a rich habits instructor. For the rest of the summer, he was my tennis coach.

"By the end of the summer you'll be winning tournaments," he said matter of factly. "You're going to learn how to think your way through matches. I'll show you how to win tournaments."

With that, we headed to the court for my first of many lessons that summer.

J.C. lined up coaches for me for basketball and baseball as well. All former pros. All nationally respected coaches. All rich habits instructors. J.C.'s reach was everywhere, it seemed. That's how it went for the rest of the summer. J.C.'s lessons, J.C.'s reading material, and J.C.'s coaches. It was overwhelming at first, but after a few days I grew to love the routine.

CHAPTER TEN

UNDERSTANDING LUCK

The next day's lesson was about luck. J.C. said it was a very important lesson because so many people don't understand luck or the different types of luck.

"Financial success is elusive. Financial success requires good luck. One of the most profound things that came out of the five-year research study, which is the backbone of my financial success, was the realization that wealthy people create their own good luck. Unsuccessful people believe that those who are wealthy and successful are just the beneficiaries of random good luck. Being in the right place at the right time kind of thinking. The reality is, successful people create their own unique type of good luck. They do certain things every day that move them forward in life and create the opportunity for luck to occur. In order to understand how the wealthy create luck, you must first understand the four types of luck that exist:

1. **Random Good Luck**
2. **Random Bad Luck**
3. **Opportunity Luck**
4. **Detrimental Luck**

RANDOM GOOD LUCK

This is a type of luck that no one has control over. It's like winning the lottery, an inheritance from an old relative you didn't even know had money, or being born into a rich family.

RANDOM BAD LUCK

When people say they have no luck, they usually mean they have no good luck. The fact is, we all experience random luck in our lives. Random luck is very democratic. It happens to everyone, rich or poor. Unfortunately, sometimes this random luck is random bad luck. Getting hit by lightning, your employer going bankrupt, or being born with some physical disability are all types of random bad luck.

OPPORTUNITY LUCK

The good luck created by the wealthy is known as opportunity luck. Opportunity luck is a byproduct of doing certain things every day. Creating good luck requires having rich habits. The rich habits are responsible for financial success. These rich habits are what set the successful apart from everyone else in life. Rich habits and opportunity luck are two sides of the same success coin. Without these rich habits, opportunity luck and success are impossible. By living these rich habits, every day, the rich process luck into their lives. When you live the rich habits, opportunity luck manifests itself. The rich habits force you to become opportunity conscious. You begin to see opportunities. Oftentimes these opportunities come dressed up in work clothes. Sometimes these opportunities appear in the form of a financial investment or an investment of your time. And sometimes opportunity luck makes its appearance in the form of an ordinary man peddling a product or idea, or even as an author trying to promote their book. Those who live the rich habits and who achieve unimaginable wealth are always the beneficiaries of opportunity luck."

J.C. loved making points by giving examples.

"Think of opportunity luck as a tree. When you live your life a certain way, when you live the rich habits, you are planting opportunity luck seeds. As you nurture your seeds, as you live the rich habits, your opportunity luck trees begin to grow. In time, your opportunity luck trees will bear fruit. Think of this fruit as a manifestation of opportunity luck. This fruit may be a raise, a promotion, a bonus, a financial windfall, a long, healthy life, good relationships, etc.

Most wealthy individuals, I found, were not even aware that they created their own luck. They just thought they were 'lucky.' J. Paul Getty was an oil tycoon back in the 1900s. When he was asked what he attributed his immense wealth to, he said: 'Some people find oil, others don't.' Even Getty thought his wealth was a matter of random good luck. For this very reason, the concept of success has been shrouded in mystery. Thus the phrase, 'the secret to financial success.' But thanks to the discoveries I made in my research, the secret to financial success is no longer a secret. The fact is, creating wealth is nothing more than processing success into your life by living the rich habits and watching opportunity luck manifest itself out of thin air.

We'll talk more about the rich habits soon.

DETRIMENTAL LUCK

Poor people create a specific type of bad luck, with their poverty habits, known as detrimental luck. Like the opportunity luck tree, there is a detrimental luck tree. When you have poverty habits, you are planting the seeds to your detrimental luck tree. You nurture this detrimental luck tree by continuing to live your life with poverty habits. In time, this tree will bear fruit. But when it does, watch out. The detrimental luck fruit that grows on your detrimental luck tree may be financial ruin, a job loss, a demotion, a heart attack, diabetes, etc. If you want to become wealthy, you need to eliminate detrimental luck and attract opportunity luck into your life. In order to do this you must have rich habits. Habits can be changed. People do it every day. It's not an impossible feat. It only takes thirty days to eliminate some of your poverty habits and introduce new rich habits. Embracing these rich habits ensures that you will attract opportunity luck and is a firewall against detrimental luck. It's like a double in baseball. By living the rich habits, you double your chances of success. By changing your habits, you change your luck, and that changes your life."

CHAPTER ELEVEN

THE IMPORTANCE OF MENTORS

"Having a mentor in life is like someone depositing millions and millions of dollars into your bank account. Mentoring is critical to success. In life, there are five places to find a success mentor:

PARENTS

Parents are often the only shot any of us have at having a mentor in life. Parents all want the best for their children. They want them to grow up to be happy and successful in life. But it doesn't just happen. Kids, left to their own devices, will seek the path of least resistance. They'll shirk their homework for pretty much anything. It's up to parents to teach their children how to be happy and successful in life."

J.C. paused and looked out across the sand and into the distance, as if straining for the right words. He seemed almost in pain.

"The fact is, parents are responsible for most of the poverty in society. Not the economy, not the government, not rich people, not big corporations, not teachers. Parents. I've gotten into a lot of fights on this topic over the years with many, many people. It's hard for some to accept that the poverty habits we pick up from our parents are responsible for our poverty. Everyone would rather blame their poverty on anyone or anything but themselves. They don't want to take individual responsibility for ending their poverty. That thinking gets them nowhere. It keeps them poor. You can't become successful if you're always blaming others for your circumstances. It's important for parents to instill in their kids the rich habit of taking individual responsibility for their lives. It's important for parents to teach their kids all the rich habits. Kids are always watching their parents and copying their behaviors and habits. If those behaviors and habits are poverty habits, the kids will pick them up and take those habits into their adult lives. Kids who learn poverty habits from their parents grow up to become unhappy, unsuccessful, and poor. Worse, they pass along those poverty habits to their children, and this cycle of poverty perpetuates itself from one generation to the next. It's the reason the poor get poorer.

Kids raised by parents who teach them rich habits grow up to become happy, successful, and wealthy. Unfortunately, those raised in rich habits households represent only about 5 percent of the population in any country. This 5 percent do not struggle financially, they have nice homes, vacation at the nicest places, and are generally well educated. The most important thing is that kids born into rich habits households pass along these habits to their children, and their children grow up to become happy, successful, and wealthy. This cycle of wealth perpetuates itself from one generation to the next, and it is the reason why the rich get richer.

Remember that success seesaw we talked about a few days ago? On one side of the seesaw are your rich habits and on the other side are your poverty habits. The key to happiness and success in life is to make sure that more than 50 percent of your daily habits are rich habits. This tips your seesaw towards a happy, successful life. When more than 50 percent of your daily habits are poverty habits, it tips the seesaw in the wrong direction, and life will be unhappy and you will struggle financially.

Parenting goes way beyond providing children with the basics. Parents need to become mentors to their children. If you want your children to grow up to be happy and successful in life, you need to become a mentor to your children. Quite frankly, the best parents are mentors to their children. They mentor their children to be more than functioning adults; they raise their children to be exceptional. They raise their children to be happy and successful in life. There is no exception to this rule. Take a look at any successful millionaire and you will find at least one parent, or some nonparent mentor, who instilled in them the rich habits."

J.C., always the master of the example, then rattled off a list of a few successful people who had a mentor-parent:

"Warren Buffet

Many probably don't know that Warren Buffet's father was a stockbroker. It's no accident that Buffet became the world's best known investor. He was mentored by his dad.

The Kennedys

Joseph Kennedy was a very successful politician who mentored sons JFK, Bobby Kennedy, and Teddy Kennedy: all very successful, famous politicians.

John Quincy Adams

John Quincy Adams was the sixth President of the United States. His father was John Adams, one of the founding fathers of America and the second President of the United States. He spent much of his youth with his father in France. His father had a great influence on him, teaching him rich habits and instilling in him a desire to learn.

The stories of parents who raised successful children all have one thing in common: mentorship. It's not an accident that their children excel in life.

TEACHERS

The best teachers are success mentors. Teachers can reinforce the mentoring children receive at home from their parents, or step in to provide the much needed success mentoring absent at home.

WORK

Finding someone at work who can act as a mentor will help ensure success in life. How do you go about finding a mentor at work? It's simple. You look for someone at work that you admire and respect and ask them to be your mentor. Let's say you find someone at work who fits the bill. Here's how you ask them to be your mentor: 'John, I've been watching you for some time and you are very good at what you do. I would like to follow in your footsteps. Would you be my mentor here at work?'

How could John say no? Unless John's a jerk, he will be very flattered and say yes. The interesting thing about successful people, something most people don't understand, is that they enjoy helping others achieve success. It's rewarding to them. They also understand that being a mentor is not a one-way street. Mentoring also helps them become a better teacher. You must really know your area of expertise to be able to teach it to someone. Being a mentor benefits both parties. Over time, your relationship with your career mentor will grow stronger. The lessons they will share with you will move beyond the workplace. Your career mentor will teach you about success both inside the workplace and in life. He or she will share with you their morality, success principles, and rich habits. They will also share with you the mistakes they've made and the life lessons they learned from those mistakes in order to help you avoid repeating their mistakes. In this way, career mentors pave the road to success with a smooth surface. They remove the rocks and potholes. They remove the detour signs. Career mentoring, outside of parent mentoring, is the most direct path to financial success.

But what if there is no one at work who fits the bill? There are other ways to find mentors in life. For example, you can join a network group. Network groups are a great way to meet new people both within and without your field of expertise. Over time, your relationships will grow stronger and you will be able to identify outstanding individuals who can act as your mentor.

Volunteering at nonprofits or civic organizations is another way to meet individuals who can become your mentors in life. Many wealthy, successful individuals sit on the boards of various nonprofit organizations or work in the numerous committees that every nonprofit has. In these nonprofits you will find many outstanding individuals who can act as your mentor. Trade groups or trade organizations are another avenue to finding a mentor in your industry. Getting involved in these trade groups will expose you to many potential mentors.

BOOKS

Many successful people attribute their success in life to self-help–success authors, such as Dale Carnegie, Earl Nightingale, or Og Mandino. These authors can act as your mentors in life, directing you, through their writing, what to do and what not to do and helping you achieve your goals. The best books for finding mentors are self-help books and biographies of successful people. You have some of them in that bag I gave you. Think of each book I gave you as a mentor.

SCHOOL OF HARD KNOCKS

When you learn rich habits through the school of hard knocks, you are essentially your own mentor. You teach yourself. You learn from your own mistakes and failures. This is the hard way, because those mistakes and failures often cost you time and money."

CHAPTER TWELVE
WEALTH AND POVERTY IDEOLOGIES

"There are two opposing schools of thought surrounding wealth and poverty. These two schools of thought are as follows:

1. The 'I Am a Victim' School of Thought and
2. The 'Individual Responsibility' School of Thought

'I AM A VICTIM' SCHOOL OF THOUGHT

This school of thought argues that poverty is outside your control. You are a victim of your circumstances. Individual responsibility, behaviors, and habits are irrelevant. Life screwed you. Circumstances beyond your control dictate your poverty. You may have been born into a poor or dysfunctional family, or you were raised in a bad neighborhood, or you chose to work in an industry that pays low wages, or you were simply the victim of random bad luck. What makes this ideology relevant is that, for a small minority, there is a small grain of truth to it. Disabilities, medical ailments, and any number of conditions can and do work against you in a random manner. Unfortunately, proponents of this ideology extrapolate these exceptions and apply them to the whole of poverty. But the reality is that poverty, for the vast majority of people, is self-inflicted. Those who embrace this victim ideology see the poor as good and the rich as evil. This ideology is nothing less than an all-out assault on the individual pursuit of success and prosperity. Its objective is to create a sense of victim status, dependence, and limited opportunity. Worse, it does nothing to help the poor. In fact, it actually contributes to poverty by rationalizing away individual responsibility for your circumstances in life.

If you are not engaged in daily self-improvement, every day, you will not improve your circumstances in life and you will remain poor. If you do not believe you can become successful, you will not improve your circumstances in life and you will remain poor. Do not buy into this 'I am a victim' ideology. Those who push this ideology either do not know any better or have an agenda to keep people poor. Many born into poverty, unfortunately, embrace this ideology and are never able to break free of poverty. Worse, it enslaves their children to a life of poverty, unhappiness, and despondency, unless they are among the lucky few who are able to find a mentor at school or at work. It perpetuates a generational cycle of poverty.

'INDIVIDUAL RESPONSIBILITY' SCHOOL OF THOUGHT

Advocates for this school of thought believe wealth and poverty are the byproduct of individual behavior, individual choices, and individual habits. They believe that you have the ability to change your circumstances and can rise above poverty if you work hard, engage in continuous lifelong self-improvement, make good choices in life, and form good habits. This school of thought believes those who continuously seek to better themselves and their circumstances create their own good luck and wealth will follow. They also believe those who do not seek to better themselves and their circumstances create their own bad luck and poverty will follow. This ideology says you are not a victim; you have the ability to change your impoverished circumstances in life and achieve unlimited wealth and success. Wealthy, successful people all embrace this ideology."

CHAPTER THIRTEEN

NEW YORK CITY

My parents and sisters had just said their good-byes and were on their way back home after spending another weekend at the shore house with J.C. and me. We watched them from the porch as they drove away. J.C. must have sensed my sadness.

"When are your friends coming?" he asked.

"Around five. Another hour or so," I responded.

"I've got a fun week planned for us."

My eyes began to light up. "What are we doing, J.C.?" I asked impatiently.

"Going to New York City for the week. I booked a hotel in midtown. We'll head out first thing in the morning. Got a party bus picking us up at 7 a.m."

The bus ride into New York was a blast. We were all excited and pent up with anticipation. J.C. booked a big suite at the Plaza right across from Central Park. We arrived at the Plaza at 9 a.m., finished unpacking our bags, had some breakfast, and then walked across the street to Central Park. There were all these horse-drawn carriages just outside the park, and J.C. rented two of them to take us around the park. The carriages were a staple at Central Park. They had a regal look to them, like something out of Buckingham Palace in England. The horses were beautiful and powerful looking.

It was a beautiful morning in New York City. The sun was shining, people were everywhere. There were vendors selling mementos, books, and all different kinds of food. Our carriage ride around the park took about an hour. We stopped every now and then when the carriage driver wanted to point something out, like the big boulders. He explained how the boulders were created by the ice age over ten thousand years ago. The ice sheets would pull all the rocks up deep from under the ground and push them along its path. He also explained how the ground beneath New York City was formed by the combination of two supercontinents crashing together a billion years ago to create the sturdy bedrock that allowed builders to construct such large skyscrapers.

When we finished our carriage ride, J.C. arranged a bike tour of Central Park. The guide took us all around the park to places the carriages couldn't go. He also gave us a history lesson, this time about the park. It was the first public park in America, built by twenty thousand Irish laborers in the mid 1800s. We stopped every now and then so J.C. could take pictures of us climbing the boulders. After the bike tour, we went to the Central Park Zoo and then strolled over to the Conservatory Garden. J.C. told us there were actually three gardens: French, Italian, and English. We walked through this huge gate called the Vanderbilt Gate and then made our way to an open area in the Italian section. It had a large lawn surrounded by tiered hedges with white crab apple trees all around it. There was this large fountain also surrounded by hedges that led up to something called a pergola. A pergola looks like a trellis, like something out of a Greek history book.

We had lunch at a famous restaurant called Tavern on the Green right inside Central Park. J.C. knew the owners and had arranged for us to have lunch there. They treated us like royalty.

After lunch, J.C. took us to the boathouse at the park and we rented some boats. We paddled around the park and were splashing water on each other the whole time. It was so much fun.

We were all tired after the boat ride and headed back to the hotel and watched a movie on this big TV in the main area of the suite. It was the first time we had ever watched a VCR movie on a TV. My friends thought it was so cool. Some of my friends fell asleep on the big couch in front of the TV, exhausted. What a day.

That night J.C. took us to a famous sports bar for dinner called Jimmy Weston's. The bar had something called cable TV, and every TV had a different sporting event going on. There was this one huge movie screen in the middle of the restaurant. It was replaying an old boxing match between Roberto Duran and Sugar Ray Leonard.

On day two, J.C. arranged to have several cabs take us downtown to a place called the South Street Seaport. J.C. walked us over to this large open platform area on the water. There were helicopters coming and going. Someone came over to J.C. and directed us all to this one large helicopter and told us to get in. My friends were flipping out, but I was petrified. J.C. sat himself in the chair right next to mine and gave me a look that said, "Don't worry, I'm right here." We had to put on these headsets to drown out the noise from the helicopter blades. After a few minutes I forgot we were high up in the air and began to take in the scenery. We spent about an hour and a half in that helicopter, but it seemed like only a few minutes. Time always flies when you're having fun.

J.C. wasn't done. Next we took a long walk along the water. We passed by the ferry that takes you to Staten Island and kept walking to a place called Battery Park. At Battery Park we caught a ferry that took us to Ellis Island. Ellis Island was where a lot of immigrants from Ireland and Italy came during the mid 1800s.

After Ellis Island, we took another ferry to the Statue of Liberty. We learned the statue was a gift from France to the U.S. We climbed these narrow stairs all the way to the top of the Statue of Liberty. We could see Staten Island, New Jersey, and the Hudson River for miles and miles. As soon as we got to the top, I became very anxious. J.C. sensed this and put his arm around me, hugging me close. I calmed down after a few minutes.

After we got back to the city from the Statue of Liberty, we walked over to the Staten Island Ferry for a trip back and forth across the Hudson. We had hot dogs and sodas on the ferry while J.C. went on about the history of the Staten Island Ferry, which dated back to the mid 1800s. He told us it was run by Cornelius Vanderbilt. Vanderbilt was a wealthy industrialist from Staten Island. We all went outside the ferry to watch it dock. J.C. took some more pictures. We made our way back to the Plaza just before dinner. J.C. thought it would be fun to order room service and watch a movie, so we did.

On day three, J.C. took us for a tour of the Empire State Building. We finished up the tour on the observation deck. I kept saying to myself, "all these heights." It was as if J.C. was intentionally adding all these activities that involved heights. The observation deck had these viewing stations around the edges of the deck. They magnified everything you looked at. My friends and I were laughing as we battled each other for the best viewing stations. So much fun. After the tour, J.C. took us to Rockefeller Plaza and we walked around for a while taking in all the sights.

Then we went to St. Patrick's Cathedral. Inside they had all this beautiful stained glass. It was the largest church any of us had ever been in.

Then it was off to the Museum of Natural History. I wasn't a museum person, but this museum had so many unusual exhibits. It was mind boggling. They had one called the Hall of Primates with life-size gorillas and one that showed how humans evolved. There was the Fossil Hall that had all these dinosaur skeletons. There was a planetarium and another area that displayed the largest meteorite in the world. We learned so much that day, but it was fun learning.

On day four, J.C. took us to Coney Island and we spent the day going on ride after ride. We all went on something called a wonder wheel, which was the biggest Ferris wheel I ever saw. Once again, I found myself high in the air with J.C. by my side, arm around my shoulder. Then we went to the aquarium at Coney Island. When we were done we were all exhausted. Even J.C. looked tired.

We headed home on day five. The party bus picked us up in the morning, and before long we were all back on J.C.'s porch talking about our amazing week in New York City. J.C. was a god to my friends and me.

CHAPTER FOURTEEN

RICH HABITS

Everyone knew about the rich habits. J.C.'s book was famous around the world. It was translated into thirty different languages and made J.C. Jobs a household name. I knew this would be one of J.C.'s most important lessons of the summer. J.C. had to spread the lessons on the rich habits and poverty habits out over that entire week.

"Our daily habits are the reason why we are rich, poor, or middle class. Forty percent of all of our daily activities are habits. This means 40 percent of the time we are all on autopilot, every day. If we have more rich habits than poverty habits, life will be good and we will be happy. If we have more poverty habits than rich habits, then life will be a struggle. Financial difficulties will arise that cause stress and make us unhappy. All of our habits are stored by the brain in the basal ganglia. This is a golf-ball size mass of tissue smack in the center of the brain. Habits save the brain work. There is very little processing power involved with respect to habits. When a habit is formed and stored in this region, the rest of the brain stops fully participating in any decision making with respect to that habit.

There are two types of daily habits:

1. **Ordinary Daily Habits and**
2. **Keystone Daily Habits**

Ordinary daily habits are simple, basic, standalone habits: the time we wake up in the morning, the route we take to work, how we hold a fork, etc. Keystone daily habits are unique daily habits. They are unique because they affect other daily habits. Keystone daily habits are like scavengers; they move around searching for and eating up other weaker, ordinary daily habits. Oftentimes, the daily habits they eliminate are daily habits that are in opposition to the keystone habit. Let me give you an example.

It's New Year's Day and one of your resolutions is to lose weight. You're about fifty pounds overweight. A close friend, who is a runner, says the fastest way to lose weight is to run. So you decide to start jogging, which is a rich habit. You hate jogging, but after doing it for a month or so, you're down ten pounds. One night you go out to a social event and someone you know compliments you on your weight loss and tells you how amazing you look. You go home that night feeling happy and motivated. You feel like you're floating on air. You're totally pumped up. The next morning you decide to cut back on junk food, a poverty habit, and stop overeating, another poverty habit. You decide you want to jog more in order to increase your weight loss, so you make a decision to cut back on your smoking, a poverty habit. You know smoking hurts your breathing and limits how fast and how far you can jog. Adopting just one keystone habit, jogging, causes the elimination of three ordinary daily habits: junk food, overeating, and smoking cigarettes. That's why keystone habits are so unique. They act as a catalyst in changing your poverty habits.

Experts debate how to change a habit, how long it takes, and even if it's possible to get rid of habits. I intentionally designed the rich habits to be keystone habits in order to maximize their effectiveness. Adopting just one rich habit will cause the elimination of two or more poverty habits. All you need to do is add one or more rich habits and your poverty habits will begin to magically disappear. This is the power of the rich habits. They tap into your emotions. No willpower is required. When you add a few rich habits to your daily routine, they chip away at your poverty habits, which gets your seesaw tipping toward success.

There are ten rich habits that, when followed, will almost guarantee you become happy and successful in life. Let's go through them, one by one.

Rich Habit #1: I Will Form Good Daily Habits and Follow These Good Daily Habits Each and Every Day

This rich habit is the most important rich habit. It is the foundation upon which all of the other rich habits were built. I like to call this rich habit the self-assessment habit. The self-assessment rich habit requires that you list all of your bad habits and then convert them to good habits. For example, spending more than an hour a day watching T.V. recreationally is a bad habit. Your new good habit is limiting yourself to one hour of recreatioinal T.V. a day."

J.C. stopped and looked at me.

"Your homework for tonight will be to list ten bad habits that you have and then convert them to good habits. Will you do that for me?"

"Sure," I responded.

J.C. turned back and resumed the lesson. "Some of the greatest historical figures worked diligently at self-assessment and self-improvement. Benjamin Franklin and George Washington even created lists of good behavioral activities to help them eliminate any defects or bad habits they thought they had. Benjamin Franklin's list is known as the '13 Virtues of Life.' He compiled this list at the age of twenty and diligently spent an entire year trying to live by those virtues. George Washington's list is known as 'The Rules of Civility and Decent Behavior.' Washington wrote this list while still a teenager. Is it an accident that these two self-improvement fanatics had enormous success in life? I don't think so.

Rich Habit #2: I Will Set a Goal for Each Day, Each Month, Each Year, and for the Long-Term. I Will Focus on My Goals Each and Every Day

Successful people set daily, monthly, annual, and long-term goals. They understand the difference between a wish and a goal. This is a pretty big topic, so we'll get more into that another day.

Rich Habit #3: I Will Engage in Self-Improvement Each and Every Day

Successful people engage in at least thirty minutes a day of self-improvement reading. They read or listen to books, articles, newsletters, etc. They study stuff that will help them do a better job. They go to seminars, attend speaking engagements, and take courses at night school. They write and do speaking engagements related to their jobs. This is the second most important rich habit. I'll spend more time on this down the road.

Rich Habit #4: I Will Devote Part of Each and Every Day in Caring for My Health

Successful people are healthy people. They exercise aerobically thirty minutes or more a day, four days a week, and stay below their 'caloric threshold.' This 'caloric threshold' is the number of calories consumed each day that will keep you at your current weight. For men this ranges from 2,000 to 2,600 calories a day. For women this ranges from 1,500 to 2,100 calories a day. I've got a separate lesson for this one too.

Rich Habit #5: I Will Devote Part of Each Day to Forming Lifelong Relationships

Successful people manage their relationships every day. Strong relationships are the currency of the successful. They use certain strategies to grow their relationships, such as: 'The Hello Call,' 'The Happy Birthday Call,' and 'The Life Event Call.' We'll talk more about this another day.

Rich Habit # 6: I Will Live Each and Every Day in a State of Moderation

Successful people live each day in moderation. They eat in moderation, spend in moderation, work in moderation, and play in moderation. The homes they live in are modest and the cars they drive are modest. They stay away from designer clothes and expensive restaurants.

Rich Habit #7: I Will Accomplish My Daily Tasks Each and Every Day. I Will Adopt a 'Do It Now' Mindset

Successful people complete at least 70 to 80 percent of the tasks on their daily to-do list. Procrastination is a poverty habit that I want to spend more time on another day.

Rich Habit #8: I Will Engage in Rich Thinking Every Day

Successful people engage in 'rich thinking.' They are upbeat, positive, and focused on achievement. This is another very important rich habit. I've got a separate lesson planned for this one for another day.

Rich Habit #9: I Will Save 10 to 20 Percent of Every Paycheck

Wealthy individuals save a minimum of 10 to 20 percent of their income and live off of the remaining 80 to 90 percent. We already talked about the 80:20 rule on the first day, so I won't beat a dead horse.

Rich Habit #10: I Will Control My Thoughts and Emotions Each and Every Day

Successful people control their thoughts and emotions, every day. This is another topic that I'll cover later on.

I looked over at Brendan. That was one of the longest lessons J.C. gave me all summer. It took us a few days to get through it. J.C. said it was the heart of everything he was teaching me that summer. I must have read his book *Rich Habits* a dozen times since that summer. It's in the back pocket of the notebook."

Brendan paged through the notebook to the end and found the book.

"Short read, Dad," he said, leafing through it.

"Yeah. J.C. said he made it short so people would read it. It only takes about three hours to get through it. You can read it on our way back home from Notre Dame if you want."

Brendan nodded. We were about halfway to Notre Dame. The notebook story was making time fly by.

"The next lesson is called 'Poverty Habits,' Dad," Brendan said.

"Ah yes, the poverty habits. Let's talk about poverty habits."

CHAPTER FIFTEEN

POVERTY HABITS

J.C. would tell me all the time that summer that the law of cause and effect dictates our wealth or poverty in life.

"Rich habits are the cause and success is the effect. Poverty habits are the cause and poverty is the effect. While it's important to know what to do in life, it's equally important to know what not to do. Knowing the rich habits only gets you halfway there. Let's go over some of the poverty habits that hold people back in life:

- You watch more than one hour of TV a day.

- You eat more than three hundred junk food calories a day.

- You drink more than two glasses of beer, wine, or hard alcohol a night.

- You don't exercise aerobically a minimum of thirty minutes a day, four days a week.

- Your relationships are on an 'as needed' basis. You only reach out to your friends to socialize or when you have problems and need their help. You don't call them just to say hello, say happy birthday, or congratulate them or console them when something happens in their lives. In other words, you pretty much ignore them except when socializing or when you need them for something.

- Procrastination is the rule rather than the exception. You don't maintain a daily to-do list, or if you do, you don't accomplish 70 percent or more of your daily to-do list each day.

- You devote very little time to your career beyond working. You don't read a minimum of thirty minutes a day of educational, self-help, or career-related reading material.

- You don't network or volunteer a minimum of five hours a month.

- You do the bare minimum at work. You have 'it's not in my job description' syndrome.

- You talk too much and don't listen enough. You violate the 5:1 rule. I'll get into that rule a little bit later.

- Oftentimes, you are putting your foot in your mouth and saying inappropriate things. You don't filter the thoughts that come out of your mouth. You say whatever is on your mind.

- You pride yourself on speaking your mind, even though it hurts other people.

- You are not generous with your time or money with respect to your relationships.

- You are a spender and not a saver. You don't save 10 to 20 percent of your net income every month. That's the 80:20 rule again.

- You spend more than you earn and your debt is overwhelming you.

- You don't control your thoughts and emotions on a daily basis. You lose your temper too often and belittle others too much. You're envious of others. We'll get more into poverty emotions later.

- You think a wish is a goal. Goals require a specific physical activity, otherwise they are just wishes, and wishes don't come true. I've got a separate lesson on goals. We'll cover that soon."

"But you smoke cigars and drink beer, J.C.," I remarked out of curiosity.

J.C. gave me a look that said "smart-ass kid," but I didn't let that deter me.

"Aren't they poverty habits?"

"Yes, they're poverty habits." J.C. reluctantly admitted. "And I hold on to them for dear life. Some poverty habits are just not worth giving up."

J.C. paused for a moment, turning his head away from me and scanning the horizon just above the crashing waves.

"Remember rich habit # 6?" J.C. asked.

I hadn't yet committed the rich habits to memory.

"Everything in moderation," J.C. blurted out. "I smoke cigars and drink beer in moderation. 'One cigar a night and you'll be all right.' 'Two beers an hour for the rest of your life.' Those are the rules I stick to for those poverty habits. If I smoke more than one cigar a day I know my body can't handle it, and if I'm out drinking at some event or party and I drink more than two beers an hour, I know I'll get drunk and that it will hurt my body and might cause me to say something I regret. Anything in excess is bad for you. Even good things like exercise. That's why that moderation rich habit is so important. It keeps your rich habits and poverty habits in line."

The boardwalk lesson was over and we made our way down the stairs of the boardwalk and back home for sports camp.

CHAPTER SIXTEEN
DAILY SELF-IMPROVEMENT

"Wealthy, successful people are fanatics when it comes to daily self-improvement. They understand that knowledge creates opportunities and opportunities lead to opportunity luck. As a result, successful people are in constant pursuit of knowledge in order to help them identify opportunities.

There are four self-improvement strategies the successful use to make themselves indispensable and invaluable to all of their relationships.

STRATEGY #1 READ

Successful, wealthy people read thirty minutes or more each day for self-improvement. They read at least two or more nonfiction books a month. They listen to audio books while commuting to work, jogging, mowing the lawn, doing the laundry, lifting weights, cleaning, washing the car, trimming the hedges, etc. They also read magazines, newsletters, newspaper articles, etc. The books, magazine articles, newsletters, or newspaper articles they read are educational, self-help, job-related, or biographies of successful people. They focus their reading on nonfiction because fiction does not help them gain the knowledge they need to be successful and make more money. By increasing their knowledge base they are able to uncover more opportunities, which translates into more money and more success. It also makes them more valuable to their employer, customers, or clients and it helps them to rise up the ladder of success.

They do this daily reading day in and day out, like brushing their teeth.

STRATEGY #2 WRITE

Successful individuals engage in writing in a number of ways: company newsletters, industry newsletters, newspaper articles, industry publications, or books. Writing helps you get noticed by others in your industry. Writing is a form of communication. Writing requires that you know your subject better than reading will allow, so you can explain it to others through your writing. When you write, you are perceived as an expert. It increases your value to your employer, customers, or clients.

STRATEGY #3 SPEAK

Speaking, like writing, is a form of communication. Speaking requires a greater understanding of a subject matter than writing or reading will provide. In a speaking engagement, you may be asked a question, and this makes it a two-way communication process. When you are 'the expert' on a speaking topic, you must really know your topic, inside and out. This requires a more detailed study that reading and writing alone won't provide. It forces you to dig deeper and expand your knowledge base and elevates your perceived expertise in the eyes of your audience, who may be fellow students, colleagues, supervisors, customers, or clients.

The best time to learn how to become a speaker is now. Start now. Join groups in school that require you to speak. Join Toastmasters, take a public speaking class, run for school president, join volunteer groups, and offer to speak at functions. Practice makes perfect. Here's something no one ever tells you about speaking—it only takes one good speaking experience to turn you into a great speaker. It's magical. It's like someone turns on a light switch in your head. The more you speak, the better you become at speaking and the closer you get to that one great speech. Being a good speaker requires four things:

1. **Speak in your own voice—be yourself.**

2. **Know your topic.**

3. **Communicate with passion.**

4. **Look at the audience. When you look at the audience, move your eyes back and forth between members of your audience, like you are watching a tennis ball move back and forth across the court. Every now and then, look in someone's eyes. That really blows them away.**

The most successful and wealthy people in the world are amazing speakers. When you learn how to speak, it dramatically increases your self-confidence.

STRATEGY #4 REPETITION

There is no better way to perfect your knowledge in an area than through repetition. Repetition in a particular area gets you closer to perfection than reading, writing, or speaking ever will. Each time you repeat a specific task in a particular area you become more efficient and more expert. Through repetition you will, in time, become a master in a particular task or subject matter. It turns into muscle memory and gets stored in that basal ganglia part of the brain we talked about earlier.

Individuals who employ all four self-improvement strategies experience the greatest success. But you can achieve a good measure of success by simply dedicating yourself, every day, to just one. Make no mistake about it; daily self-improvement is not easy. But the by-product is the discovery of otherwise hidden opportunities that are always present, always right in front of everyone's eyes, waiting to be seen and taken advantage of in life."

J.C. had an example for every occasion.

"I like to use the following example to best explain how these strategies work: Imagine for a moment that you find yourself surrounded by trees. These trees are a metaphor for opportunities.

Do you know what a metaphor is?"

I didn't, so I shook my head no.

"A metaphor is like a symbol. It represents something. A trophy is a symbol of winning, so I guess you can say a trophy is a type of metaphor for being a winner. Now imagine off to the side of these trees is a hill. This hill is a metaphor for daily self-improvement. As you climb higher and higher up the hill, as you engage in more and more self-improvement, you realize you were in a forest, and what you now see are not just individual trees but a forest: a forest of opportunities. Climbing that hill, engaging in daily self-improvement, allows you to see more opportunities in life. Those who see more opportunities in life and act on them make more money and become more successful."

J.C. was in rare form. I never saw him so animated. I asked him why he seemed so pumped up, after we finished our review, and he told me it was because he had stumbled on the daily self-improvement strategy of reading way before he knew anything about the rich habits. He said it was the only rich habit he had stumbled on in life. He said that one rich habit enabled him to pass the twenty-two hour CPA exam, get his master's degree, and get all sorts of other professional licenses. Most important, he said, it helped him rise above poverty. J.C. said that as a young man, he had always thought of himself as dumb, stupid, and below the average intelligence that was required in life in order to be successful. He thought he'd always be poor. Yet this one single rich habit dragged him out of poverty and out of his poverty thinking. J.C. said when he completed his rich habits research, years later, he only then realized how important that one self-improvement rich habit was in achieving success in life. It was the one common denominator in every wealthy, successful person he interviewed in his study. They all engaged in daily self-improvement.

CHAPTER SEVENTEEN
RICH ETIQUETTE

The summer was half over already. It was just flying by. I had learned so much already from J.C. My tennis game was at another level. I was actually giving J.C. a run for his money on the tennis court. One day I took four games from him in a set. I also learned how to dribble with both hands and without looking at the ball, and I was throwing strikes, fielding balls, and making contact with the bat without giving it a thought. The fundamentals that so many of my friends struggled with had become routine for me that summer. Mere habits.

As we stepped off the porch on our way to the boardwalk, J.C. said he wasn't sure if we were going to be able to get through the next lesson because it was one of the long ones.

"I'm gonna take this one on a fast ride, so I need you to really listen and focus. There's a lot of meat on today's bone." J.C. adjusted his glasses and began to teach.

"You have to know how to act and how to do certain things when you're around people. Successful, wealthy people have mastered certain rules of etiquette that help them in social settings.

COMMUNICATING WITH PEOPLE

You're going to meet a lot of people in life. I found there's a common thread that runs through everyone. They are single-mindedly focused on themselves. Most people are thinking about one thing during every conversation—themselves. Everyone thinks they are the most important person in the world. It's a human tendency to be selfish, and this shows up everywhere, including when we are carrying on a conversation with people. It's a very important concept to grasp. It was in that book I gave you by Dale Carnegie called *How to Win Friends and Influence People*. You'll want to review that book again after we're done with today's lesson. When you run into these new people in life you need a plan, a process to help you turn every relationship into gold. Part of that process is to learn as much about your relationships as possible, and you do that by asking questions about their life. Get to know them. Always focus on the other person and resist that human tendency to put yourself first. Make being unselfish in conversations a rich habit by asking these questions to every new person you meet in life."

J.C. then rattled off a list of the types of questions to ask of every person with whom you want to grow a relationship:

- "Basic contact information: name, address, phone number, etc.

- Are they married?

- If yes, what is their spouse's name?

- Do they have any children?

- If so, what are their names?

- What's their birthday?

- Where do they live? Do they like where they live?

- Do they have any hobbies?

- What schools did they go to? Did they go to college or graduate school?

- What schools did their spouse and children attend?

- What are they most proud of?

- Do they know any celebrities or important people? Who?

- What do they do for a living?

- What does their spouse do for a living?

- Do they like to read? If so, what do they like reading? Who's their favorite author?

- Do they like music? Who's their favorite band, singer, etc.?

- If their spouse or children work, what do they do, where do they work?

- Political affiliation?

- Religious affiliation?

- Where did they live before their current home?

- Do they like to play sports? If so, what and when, and do they play any sports now?

- Do they drink alcohol? If so, what do they drink?

- What are their favorite foods?

- What type of car do they drive?

- What are their goals?

- What groups, nonprofits, or community organizations are they affiliated with?

- Where do they like to vacation?

- Do they travel? If so, where have they been?

- What did their parents do for a living?

- Where did they grow up?

- Who are their favorite celebrities?

- What licenses or professional designations do they have?

- What are they really good at in life?

- Do they exercise? If so, what do they do?

Last thing. Always look everyone in the eye and smile a lot.

HOW TO EAT

Believe it or not, most people don't know how to eat. You're going to have to go to many social events during your life, and you need to know how to eat properly. Let's go down the list:

- As soon as you sit in your chair, take the napkin off the table and drape it over your lap.

- Never begin eating until everyone has their meal in front of them.

- Never chew with your mouth open.

- Never talk while you're chewing your food.

- Never dip any food you're eating into a sauce everyone is using.

- Don't wolf down your food. Eat at the same pace as everyone else at the table.

- Never hold a spoon, fork, or knife with your fist. There's a certain way to hold utensils. I'll show you how later on today.

- Never make gestures while your utensils are in your hands.

- Never reach for anything like salt and pepper. Always ask someone to pass things like that.

- Don't slouch at the table. Sit straight up.

- After the meal, excuse yourself and go to the bathroom and make sure you don't have any food in your teeth. I always carry a toothpick in my wallet just for this reason.

HOW TO DRESS

You have to learn how to dress in life. There's a certain way to dress for work and job interviews. You're going to go to all sorts of social events like weddings, formal dinners, informal dinners, engagement parties, wakes, funerals, birthday parties, picnics, etc. You need to know how to dress. Here's a basic rundown:

- **Work and Job Interviews** — Some professions have special-purpose clothing like construction, roadwork, electricians, etc. If you work in an office, dress like your boss or your boss's boss. In some offices it's business casual, in others it's a suit and tie for men. For woman it's slacks, or skirts with open collars. Heels or no heels are OK.

- **Weddings, Wakes, Funerals** — In most cases this will be a suit and tie for men. For women it's the same as work clothes, but many women like to wear more formal outfits. Always ask someone in advance about the dress code. Some cultures have specific dress codes for weddings. You just need to be aware of that.

- **Formals** — Usually formals are called black-tie optional. This means you have a choice of wearing a suit with a tie or a tuxedo with a bow tie. Both cases require dark shoes. Sometimes the formal can be a white-tie formal. White-tie means black tailcoat, white wing-collar shirt, white bow tie, and black shoes for men. For women, it's a long formal gown or short cocktail dress or a dressy long skirt and top, usually worn with heels. White-tie events are very rare.

INTRODUCING YOURSELF

In life you will have many opportunities to meet new people. The more successful you become, the more new people you'll meet. These meetings represent an incredible opportunity to develop valuable relationships that can benefit you down the road. Some may be your next employer, future spouse, next best friend, future co-worker, next mentor, an investor, or a future business partner. There are five basic rules to making introductions:

1. Smile.

2. Firm handshake.

3. Make eye contact.

4. Tell them who you are, why you're here, and who you know at the event.

5. Ask questions about the person you are introducing yourself to. We already covered that, so let's move on.

GOOD MANNERS

I know your mom and dad probably beat this stuff into you, but this is one dead horse I think I'll beat just a little more.

There are some basic good manners you need to have in public settings that I want you to make a habit of:

1. **Treat everyone you meet with respect.**

2. **Don't judge anyone by how they are dressed.**

3. **Say 'please' and 'thank you' often.**

4. **Never criticize, complain, or condemn and never smirk, roll your eyes, or frown when someone else is talking, even if you disagree.**

5. **Never brag.**

6. **Find a reason to praise.**

7. **Never lose your temper.**

8. **Never get drunk.**

9. **Stay positive and never negative.**

10. **Introduce your spouse, friends, colleagues, etc. to people you know at social events.**

I have a short pamphlet on etiquette that I'm going to give you. After breakfast read it and take notes on things I didn't cover."

When we got back to the house, J.C. made breakfast; he spoke and I wrote. After breakfast I went upstairs to my bedroom and did as J.C. asked. I scanned over Dale Carnegie's book, read the etiquette pamphlet he had given me, and added to my notes some details we didn't cover. This took a few hours. I laid down on my bed when I was done and soon fell fast asleep. It was just past noon when I woke to the clanging of pots and pans down in the kitchen. I made my way down to see what J.C. was doing.

"Making us a nice meal for dinner," J.C. said over his shoulder as I entered the kitchen.

J.C. had this apron on that said "I Have Van Gogh's Ear for Cooking" on the front. My dad said what made J.C. so special was that, despite his enormous wealth and fame, he remained humble and down to earth. He loved to try to make people laugh or feel better about themselves. That's why he was loved by millions. My dad said J.C. used to travel to China a lot for speaking engagements and training gigs, and within a few weeks of coming back home all these gifts would start arriving from China. Ceramic teapots, dried noodles from some place in Rudong, and Mao buttons. One person, who was in the comic book business in China, had sent a custom-made comic book with pictures of J.C. on each page accompanied by one of his famous sayings, quips, or lessons.

J.C. handed me a piece of paper which had a diagram of a table that was set for ten.

"Here. Follow that diagram and set the table for dinner tonight. Everything you need is in that cabinet." J.C. pointed to a large cabinet against the wall in the dining room.

So I set the table just like the picture. When I was done I shuffled into the kitchen.

"All done?" J.C. asked.

"Yep," I said proudly.

"Let's see the damage," J.C. said with a wry smile.

J.C. took one look at the table and burst out laughing. He was laughing so hard I thought he was gonna have a heart attack or something.

"Last I checked there was just two of us," J.C. coughed out the words, laughing.

I had set the table for ten. Just like the diagram.

"The diagram," I told J.C., "has ten settings."

J.C. looked over the diagram, shook his head up and down, and then proceeded to hit himself on the side of his head with his hand. "You're right. My bad. Evidently, the apprentice has become the master," J.C. said with a rolling laugh. "You taught me a lesson today about effective communication. Maybe it's a lesson for both of us."

When we were done re-setting the table, we headed out for afternoon sports camp. After sports camp I helped J.C. with dinner. We brought all the food out to the table.

"We're gonna do a little role playing. Make believe we're at a wedding. You don't know me and I don't know you. And here I am sitting right across from you. A complete stranger. Get to know me. Show me some etiquette."

During dinner I started asking J.C., the stranger, all sorts of questions about his life, his family, his job. J.C. would stop the role playing when I did something wrong, like picking up the wrong fork or chewing while I talked or not looking him straight in the eye. Stuff like that until I got it right. Dinner that night lasted many hours.

CHAPTER EIGHTEEN
THE 5:1 RULE

As we stepped off the porch and made our way toward the boardwalk, J.C. said that today's lesson would be one of the shortest lessons all summer. But, he said, short did not mean unimportant.

"Most people never listen. They are too busy thinking about what they want to say while the other person is talking. There is a reason life gave us two ears and only one mouth. Only when we truly listen to what the other person is saying will we be able to build strong, valuable relationships. Everyone thinks, all the time, about themselves. Successful people understand this human frailty. Listening to someone makes them feel important and valuable. When people believe that you think they are important and valuable, they will like you. They will want to spend time with you. Everyone wants to be perceived as important and valuable. They will attach themselves, like a leech, to anyone who is a good listener or makes them feel better about themselves. Good listeners have more friends, more business relationships, and stronger relationships.

"The 5:1 rule is really very simple," J.C. said. "You listen for five minutes and talk for one minute. That's it. Listen more than you talk. When you listen to what the other person is saying you learn more about the other person. You gain a better understanding of them, their problems, and their wants, needs, and desires in life. One of the books I gave you was that *How to Win Friends and Influence People* book. That's a very important book about understanding what makes people tick. Life is all about rising above your self-interest and getting into the habit of treating the other person as important. Successful people treat other people like they are the most important person in the world. When you make that a habit, you own them. They become your biggest ally in life. They will take on risks to help you reach your goals in life. They will enlist others to help you get what you want in life. They will climb mountains for you. And all you have to do is ask questions and listen."

CHAPTER NINETEEN

THE ANATOMY OF A GOAL

J.C. handed me a piece of paper as we approached the boardwalk and had me read it. It was John F. Kennedy's famous "Decision to Go to the Moon" speech:

"First, I believe that this nation should commit itself to achieving the goal, before this decade is out, of landing a man on the moon and returning him safely to the earth. No single space project in this period will be more impressive to mankind, or more important for the long-range exploration of space; and none will be so difficult or expensive to accomplish. We propose to accelerate the development of the appropriate lunar space craft. We propose to develop alternate liquid and solid fuel boosters, much larger than any now being developed, until certain which is superior. We propose additional funds for other engine development and for unmanned explorations—explorations which are particularly important for one purpose which this nation will never overlook: the survival of the man who first makes this daring flight. But in a very real sense, it will not be one man going to the moon—if we make this judgment affirmatively; it will be an entire nation. For all of us must work to put him there."

"Big dreams. That's what that was," J.C. said emphatically, arms spraying out in both directions. "Dreams, backed by goals, bring clarity. They help us focus on what's important. Goals help us to focus on accomplishing our dreams. Goals help bring clarity to what we are trying to accomplish in life. Goals work like a magnifying glass, directing the sunlight. Goals help focus our activities. Being clear about what we want helps us eliminate activities that are time wasters. When we know exactly what we want, time wasters become obvious. Time wasters are things that do nothing to get us closer to realizing our goals or dreams. We can also apply that 80:20 rule we talked about before to goal setting. Studies have shown that 80 percent of all activities are time wasters and that only 20 percent of our activities actually help move us closer to realizing our goals and dreams in life. Only when we set clear, well-defined goals will we begin to see which activities get us closer to our goals and which do not. Over time, we can eliminate 80 percent of those time-waster activities. If you're doing something that does not help you get closer to your goals, it's a time waster.

Whatever your goal, you can get there so long as you are willing to do the work that is necessary to accomplish your goals. Far too many individuals never achieve their goals. Many who fail to reach their goals simply give up on goal setting altogether. They quit out of frustration or they lose confidence in the goal-setting process. Why do so many people fail to achieve their goals? At the heart of the problem is the fact that many who set what they think are goals are not setting goals at all. They are, instead, making a wish. Wishes are not goals. What sets a wish and a goal apart are two things:

1.   Action—some physical activity—and

2.   100 percent achievability.

Wishes are wishes because there's no physical activity and no certainty. Goals become goals only when physical activity is required to achieve the goals and there is no doubt you can do the activities required. Let me give you an example.

A typical goal setter may establish a goal of making a certain amount of income for the year. They may even list this income dollar amount as a 'goal.' As the year moves along they soon begin to realize that they will not get close to reaching the income goal. This usually occurs midyear. At that point, most give up on the goal out of frustration. Feelings of inadequacy, failure, poor work ethic, and lack of focus begin to filter into their minds as a result of missing the goal. That's too bad, because the failure in achieving the goal has little to do with work ethic or focus or competence. Instead, it has everything to do with misinterpreting a wish for a goal." J.C. then went into preacher mode and summed it up with a roar: "A goal is only a goal when it requires some physical action. When you define the activity you define your goal.

Now let's dissect exactly what makes a goal a goal. The anatomy of a goal is similar to the anatomy of an artichoke. The artichoke represents the wish, the leaves are the variables, and the heart is the action that is required—your goal. In order to get to the heart of the artichoke you need to peel back the leaves. Identifying the goal inside your wish is no different. You need to peel back the leaves of your wish to get to the heart of the wish—the actions required. Once you identify the actions required, you have your goals. The only remaining issue is whether or not you have the ability to perform the actions required."

J.C. then summarized the goal-finding process:

"There are four steps to finding the goal inside every wish:

- **Step #1 — Make a wish.**

- **Step #2 — Define each variable.**

- **Step #3 — Identify the specific daily activities or actions you must take.**

- **Step #4 — Is the goal 100 percent achievable?"**

J.C. then launched into another one of his famous examples.

"At one of my first rich habits training seminars many, many years ago, I was approached by an attendee who was a very successful insurance agent. He confided in me that he had failed, for three consecutive years, to come close to achieving his goal of increasing his firm's life insurance commissions by $100,000 a year. He came to my training session because he was about to give up on that goal when he came across one of my goal training ads in the local newspaper. So he decided to attend my goal training seminar. Once the lesson was over he realized that the $100,000 goal was not a goal at all but a wish. We met later in the week in an effort to peel the artichoke and find the goal inside his wish following my four-step process:

Step #1 Make a wish.

The wish is $100,000 in additional life insurance commissions.

Step #2 Define each variable.

Life insurance policies required: Average commissions per policy = $2,000. Number of policies required = 50 policies. Meetings required to close one case = approximately 10 and a half meetings. That means you need to get 250 meetings. Prospecting calls required to obtain a meeting = 10. That means you need to make 2,500 prospecting calls.

Step #3 Define actions or activities that are required in order to meet each variable.

Action = Making ten prospecting calls per day.

Step #4 Can you perform the activity?

Can you make ten calls per day, day in and day out?

I asked the insurance agent if it was possible to make an additional 10 prospecting calls per day. Can you do the activity? He laughed and said of course he could. He would have to prepare by buying a database of names, developing a script, and then hiring someone to make the prospecting calls. We did the math and the cost of the database was less than $1,000. The cost to hire someone to make the calls was about $5,000. Investment = $6,000, plus time and effort in meeting and closing the contracts.

The insurance agent went on to achieve his goal. In fact, he hit his goal within six months. After a year he exceeded his goal and made $150,000 in additional life insurance commissions."

J.C. looked over to me with that "I'm not done yet look," and then summarized that part of the lesson.

"In order to turn a wish into a goal you will need to start with a wish. A wish becomes a goal only when you specifically define the action steps that must be accomplished in order for your wish to come true. These action-based steps become your goals. OK, I think I beat that horse enough."

J.C. then moved on to the next section of the lesson.

"Successful people use a five-step goal-setting process to help them achieve 100 percent of their goals:

- **Long-Term Wish — These are big dreams you'd like to come true within a five-year period. Create a plan for accomplishing each wish and define the goals that will get you there. Example: I will buy a house in five years. In order for this wish to come true, you set a goal of saving $12,000 a year for five years. You then set a goal of saving $1,000 per month to help get you there. In order to save $1,000 per month you have to reduce expenses and you have to make sure you deposit $250, each pay period, into a separate savings account.**

- **Next-Year Wish — These are the wishes you set for next year. They get you closer to achieving your long-term wish. For example, accumulating $24,000 in two years.**

- **Current-Year Wish — Similar to next-year wish, only shorter. For example, saving $12,000 in the current year toward the purchase of your home.**

- **Monthly Wish** — An example would be saving $1,000 each month toward the purchase of the home.

- **Goal** — This is your action-based goal. This would be reducing expenses and setting aside $250 each pay period. In order to reach your goal of saving $250 each pay period, you will need to change your behavior and make some difficult choices in life. Where can you cut back? Do you buy your lunch every day? If you made your lunch at home and brought it in to work you could save some money every day. Do you clip coupons? If you don't, then clipping coupons is another way to save money. Do you go out to restaurants? If you do, then you have the choice to go to restaurants less frequently or patronize BYOB restaurants. Cut back on buying new clothes or buy good used clothes from goodwill stores. Many wealthy people in my study did just that. The point is, there are always ways to cut back on your expenses. You just need to find them."

We then went over some of the tools successful people use to help them achieve their goals, and J.C. then helped me create the following goal chart during breakfast:

Tool # 1 Goal Chart

GOAL CHART

ACTION GOAL	MONTHLY WISH	CURRENT YEAR WISH	NEXT YEAR WISH	LONG-TERM WISH
SAVE $250 / WEEK	SAVE $1,000 / MONTH	SAVE $12,000 THIS YEAR	ACCUMULATE $24,000 BY END OF YEAR	BUY HOME
10 CALLS / DAY	CLOSE 4 LIFE CASES / MONTH	$100,000 IN LIFE INSURANCE COMMISSIONS	$200,000 IN ACCUMULATED COMMISSIONS	$500,000 IN ACCUMULATED COMMISSIONS

Tool # 2 Daily Affirmations

"Wealthy, successful people create daily affirmations that are directly related to their goals. In order for an affirmation to work, it needs to meet the following formula:

Present Tense + Action Goal

Using the insurance agent example:

'I Make' = Present Tense. '10 Prospecting Calls Today' = The Action Goal.

Tool # 3 Vision Boards

You follow up your daily affirmations with something called a vision board. A vision board is an actual picture of a goal you are pursuing. Using the insurance agent example, the vision board would be a picture of you making phone calls. Vision boards only work if they are directly tied to the goals you are working towards."

CHAPTER TWENTY

"We are only as successful as the people we spend the most time with. Wealthy, successful people associate primarily with other wealthy, successful people. Poor people associate primarily with other poor people. If you want to stay out of poverty, you need to change who you associate with. You have to evaluate each of your relationships and determine if they are a rich relationship or a poverty relationship.

Rich relationships share the following characteristics:

- They are happy.

- They are successful.

- They associate with other successful people.

- They have a lot of relationships. A thousand or more is typical. They develop these relationships over time through networking, volunteering, etc. We'll cover that later when in the rich relationship lesson.

- They have more rich habits than poverty habits.

- They are positive, upbeat, and optimistic.

- Their life is calm.

- They get along with many different types of people.

- They don't gossip about others.

- They inspire others by encouraging them and motivating them to pursue their goals and dreams.

- They are very enthusiastic.

- They avoid victim thinking and they take responsibility for their circumstances in life.

Poverty relationships share the following characteristics:

- They are unhappy.

- They struggle at work. They don't like their job, their boss, or their colleagues, and this causes them to struggle to maintain a job.

- They have more poverty habits than rich habits.

- They are negative, down, and pessimistic.

- Their life seems to be in constant turmoil. They are constantly putting out fires.

- They are always fighting with family, friends, or colleagues.

- They gossip.

- **They are dream killers.**

- **They lack enthusiasm.**

- **They are depressed or sad a lot.**

- **They have a 'poor, poor me' victim attitude. They don't take personal responsibility for their circumstances in life. Someone, some group, or some thing is responsible for their circumstances in life.**

We all have rich relationships and poverty relationships. But how many you have will determine how successful you will be. Visualize that seesaw again. How many poverty relationships and rich relationships does your relationship seesaw have? In order to get it tipping in the right direction, more than half of your relationships need to be rich ones. There are a number of steps you need to take to get it tipping in the right direction:

Step #1 List all of your relationships — Take out a pad and pencil and list every one of your relationships in the first column.

Step #2 Identify 'influence relationships' — In the next column, identify how much time you spend with each relationship. Those you spend more than an hour a week with are considered influence relationships. Influence relationships have either a positive or negative influence on you and your life.

Step #3 Score your relationships — In the third column, put a plus sign next to each name if they are a rich relationship or a minus sign if they are a poverty relationship.

Step #4 Tip your seesaw — Once you've identified all the pluses and minuses, the next step is to limit the time you spend with your poverty relationships to less than one hour a week and increase the time you spend with your rich relationships to more than an hour a week.

Step #5 Seek out rich relationships — Make a list of individuals you may or may not know, who are not on your list, but who fall into the rich relationship category. Seek to spend an hour or more a week with them. Think about each relationship you want to grow as if it were a tree. Your goal in life is to grow each relationship tree. Every time you communicate and interact with your relationships you grow the roots to your relationship tree deeper. You want each tree to be the size of a redwood at the end of your life.

There are four strategies that will help you build strong, valuable relationships:

HELLO CALL

The hello call is about gathering information. You want to learn as much as you can about each of your relationships. We already went over the questions you want to ask all of your relationships in the etiquette lesson.

HAPPY BIRTHDAY CALL

To each of us, our birthdays are important. When you wish someone a happy birthday it says to them that they are important to you. Happy birthday calls keep each one of your relationships on life support. At least once a year you keep the relationship alive. A phone call is a good way to wish someone a happy birthday because it gives you an opportunity to talk with them and gather more information. Happy birthday calls get the roots to your relationship tree a little deeper. Wherever you go, carry around a notepad, and when you meet anyone you want to get to know, don't be afraid to ask them their birthday. Then be sure to write it down in your notepad and transfer it to some reminder system. This way you will never forget anyone's birthday. I've been following this rich habit for years, and I found that about 5 to 10 percent of the people I call on their birthday will eventually reciprocate and call me on my birthday. This reciprocal happy birthday call takes your relationships off life support and grows the roots to your relationship tree deeper.

LIFE-EVENT CALL

These calls are made to family, friends, clients, customers, patients, work colleagues, or any contact you value in order to recognize a particular event that occurred in their life. An example would be if someone you know had a baby, a graduation in the family, got a promotion or a new job, or experienced a death or some illness. Life-event calls put your relationships on steroids. They grow the roots to the relationship tree deeper and faster than any other relationship-building strategy.

NETWORKING

Developing a networking process is critical to success. When you network the right way you gain friends, customers, clients, and success partners, and that translates into more success in life and more money. Successful people are master networkers. To the wealthy, relationships are like gold. It is the currency of the wealthy. Here's how you go about creating a networking process:

- Join networking groups — Business Network International is the most popular, but you can create your own networking group.

- Join boards of local businesses — Reach out to your clients, customers, business partners, and local business community and ask if they have an advisory board. If they do, offer your services as a board member. If they don't, help them set one up.

- Join civic groups — Lions Club, Rotary Club, chambers of commerce, Optimist International, etc. There are many business and nonbusiness civic groups who are looking for members. These groups often refer business to one another.

- Become a speaker — Speaking engagements are probably the most efficient networking tool available. One speaking engagement can mean ten, twenty, or a hundred new relationships. Since many individuals fear public speaking, speaking will set you apart from the masses and you will be viewed as an expert.

- Join a nonprofit group board or committee — Nonprofit groups are one of the most valuable resources for all types of referrals. You gain an opportunity to showcase your skills and develop long-lasting relationships. Referrals come from every direction: board members, committee members, vendors, donors, and beneficiaries of the organization. Very often, nonprofit board members are successful, wealthy individuals who have many strong, powerful relationships. When you join a nonprofit, the people you meet will eventually open up their address books and grant you access to many of their valuable relationships.

- Write — Writing sets you apart from your competition. As you develop your arsenal of articles, you close the credibility gap in the eyes of customers, clients, patients, work colleagues, or business partners. When you get your work published, it allows you to reach out to hundreds and maybe thousands of people, which makes it another efficient networking tool. Writing also sharpens your knife. It improves your technical skills and makes you more competent in your field or industry. When you increase your technical skills, your eyes and ears open up to opportunities that you never saw before but were there all along.

- **Socializing — Periodically reach out to your relationships and ask them to breakfast, lunch, or dinner, or just ask them if they want to grab a few drinks at a local pub. These casual get-togethers are actually the most effective way to grow your relationships."**

CHAPTER TWENTY-ONE

J.C. AT WORK

J.C.'s ramped up sports camp alternated between tennis, baseball, and basketball. Basketball sometimes involved a forty-five minute commute to the Rutgers gym in New Brunswick. For two hours J.C. had one of the assistant coaches of the men's basketball team run me through all sorts of drills. We always finished up with two hundred foul shots followed immediately by a game of around the world. The game ended when I was able to shoot my way from one side of the court to the other without missing. After a few weeks I was able to make it all the way around without a missed shot.

We were just wrapping up another afternoon basketball session. We gathered our things, said our good-byes to the assistant coach, and headed out the gym door. J.C. put his arm around me on our way to the car.

"A little change in the old routine tomorrow," J.C. said matter-of-factly. "We're headed to D.C. for a speaking engagement."

J.C. opened the back door of the station wagon and we threw our gym bags in the car. "I usually don't do speaking engagements during the summer, but I made an exception this year."

My Dad said J.C. was a world-famous speaker. He had spoken on every continent, even at the Amundsen–Scott South Pole Station in Antarctica.

"This one's a short gig," he said. "Just a few hours. We'll spend a day touring the monuments and seeing the sights. You'll need a pressed shirt and pants and your good shoes. We're going to take the RV. "

J.C.'s custom-made RV had everything. A kitchen, bath with a shower, fold-down bunk beds, huge captain chairs in the front that converted into beds, a collapsible desk, and a large twenty-inch TV with a VCR to watch movies, just like at the Plaza Hotel. J.C. said he had spent an entire week in that RV this past February just to see if it could be done. J.C. took my friends and me for a short ride in the RV earlier in the summer during one of my off weeks. Now we were going on a long trip in it. I couldn't wait for tomorrow to come.

We were on the road by five a.m. It was a short five-hour drive for me. J.C. folded out the passenger seat and let me sleep most of the way. We got to D.C. around 10 a.m. and pulled into an entrance way in front of this big white building.

I looked at J.C. "Is that the White House?!"

J.C. lowered his window and handed the guard a piece of paper. The guard smiled at J.C.

"It's good to see you again, Mr. Jobs. How's the family?"

"Everyone's great, Kevin. I've got one with me for the summer." I waved to the guard mechanically while staring at the White House, still in disbelief.

"They're expecting you, Mr. Jobs."

"Come on, Kevin. How many times do I have to tell you, it's J.C."

The guard kept smiling as he waved us through the security gate. We pulled into the back of the White House. J.C. seemed to know exactly where to go. Someone came out and J.C. gave her the keys to the RV. We made our way to the front. Another guard met us and ushered us into this huge room packed mostly with kids about my age, with a few adults scattered here and there.

J.C. leaned over to me. "They're all from Key Academy. That's where the president's granddaughter goes to school."

We barely stepped foot inside the room before we were greeted by the president and the First Lady. The president gave J.C. a big hug and the First Lady gave him a big kiss. J.C. introduced me and they both shook my hand.

"Thanks so much for doing this, J.C.," the president said.

"They're so excited to meet the famous J. C. Jobs," the First Lady gushed as she locked both of her arms around J.C.'s right arm and marched us toward the front of the stage. I followed close behind.

For the next three hours, with a few breaks here and there, J.C. talked about the rich habits, the poverty habits, the success seesaw, opportunity luck, detrimental luck, and a bunch of other stuff he'd been teaching me all summer. When he was done we had lunch with the president, the First Lady, their granddaughter, some of the students, and a few of the teachers. They sat J.C. and me down next to the president, who was seated at the head of this long table, and his granddaughter, who sat to my left. His granddaughter asked me what it was like to have a grandpa like J.C. I told her all about my summer, the lessons, sports camp, the off week to New York, and our trip here in the RV.

"You're so lucky. I wish I could do that."

I asked her all sorts of questions about her life, her school, her hobbies, and her birthday. I asked her for her contact info so I could wish her a happy birthday. She thought that was sweet and asked me for mine. We still talk to each other a few times a year to this day.

We were talking for a while until the president broke in.

"So what's J.C. teaching you this summer?"

I was more than a little surprised that he knew about my summer with J.C.

Before I could even get a word out he asked, "What books does he have you reading? Let me guess," he continued. "*How to Win Friends and Influence People, Think and Grow Rich, The Power of the Subconscious Mind*? Oh, and *Rich Habits*, of course."

Both he and J.C. started to laugh. I just smiled and nodded my head up and down.

The president continued. "Do you know how many millionaires J.C. created?"

I didn't know, so I said, "No, how many?"

"Millions," the president said. "Millions around the entire globe."

The president quizzed me about the rich habits and J.C.'s success strategies during lunch and, in between, I asked him about his job, his hobbies, and if he played sports. Pretty much all the things J.C. taught me to ask.

After lunch the First Lady gave J.C. and me a private tour of the White House. We finished up at the Oval Office. The president was there with a few very important looking men dressed in suits. J.C. later told me they were his chief of staff, some senator from Minnesota, and a banker from New

York named Sandy Weill. The president introduced us and Sandy Weill, the banker, asked me if I knew anything about saving money. I told him about the 80:20 rule, how saving is different from investing, and a few other things J.C. had taught me that summer.

J.C. later told me how proud he was of me and that I had made a great impression on Mr. Weill.

"Don't you work for a bank, Dad?" Brendan interrupted.

"Yep. Thanks to J.C. After our trip to D.C. he told me to send everyone we met a letter thanking them for meeting with us. Mr. Weill wrote back and we stayed in touch over the years. J.C. even set up a few get-togethers with Mr. Weill and another man by the name of Jamie Dimon. Lunches in New York City, mostly. I interned with Mr. Dimon during college, and when I graduated Mr. Dimon recruited me to work in their management trainee program. He had a falling out with Mr. Weill a few years later and left the company. When he became the CEO of JP Morgan, I sent him a personal letter congratulating him, a rich habit I learned that summer from J.C. He called me a few days after getting the letter and offered me a job there. Now I run their financial services division in the U.S."

We spent that night in the Lincoln Bedroom. I couldn't believe we were actually sleeping in the White House. We were both lying on the bed with books we were reading when I turned to J.C. and asked, "How do you know the president?"

J.C. set his book down on his lap and took a deep breath.

"Before he was the president, he was one of my best rich habits trainers. For years he taught thousands the rich habits. We became best friends. He ran into a fella in one of the training sessions who was a political campaign manager. They hit it off, and before long Ron was running for office. Eventually he became a governor of California and then president. I spend a lot of time in the White House."

"Mom told us your picture is hanging in the Oval Office. Is that true?"

"Yep," was all J.C. said.

"Yep? That's it. Yep? Come on, J.C. Why is your picture hanging in the Oval Office?" I pleaded with him.

"You know bragging is a poverty habit?" J.C. responded.

"I don't care. I've got to know."

J.C. smiled. "OK. Well, like I said, Ron was one of my best trainers. He was one of the first actors I had in one of my training classes. He was a real go-getter. We became close friends and he started bringing in other actors for me to train. Eventually, he joined our training program and helped grow our business on the West Coast. Somewhere along the line he got bitten with the politics bug. When he was running for governor he kind of had me on his team to help him get elected. I'd write some of his speeches, give him advice on certain issues. Politicians like to call them policy issues. Well, so, I'd give him direction by highlighting certain policy issues that I thought were important and let him know which ones weren't important. As it turns out, he gets elected and I kept advising him. We talked just about every day. I did the same when he ran for president, and I'll be damned if he didn't get elected. He considered me his main mentor in life and wanted everyone to know it, so he hung a picture of me up in the Oval Office."

"Wow. That's such a cool story, J.C."

"Yeah. It is." J.C. then immediately changed the subject.

"You know," he said, "the president was very impressed with you."

"He was?" I replied, surprised.

"Yep. He said you had great manners. He was watching you talk to his granddaughter. He said you asked her a lot of questions and kept looking her in the eye. You see," J.C. went on, "you never know who's watching. In time this stuff I'm teaching you will become second nature. Like old habits," J.C. said. "I'm proud of you. You did great today. You're one of the best students I ever had."

J.C. paused for a moment. "I'm really enjoying this summer with you." He smiled and returned to his book, and I smiled back and returned to mine.

I hardly slept that night. I felt like I was the luckiest kid in the world. I kept replaying the day over and over again in my head until my brain and body just shut down. I think J.C. must have been going through the same thing because we both slept in that morning and didn't get going until just before noon the next day. J.C. took me for a tour of the city. We hit all the sights—the Washington Monument, the Lincoln Monument, the zoo—and we even got a private tour of the Capitol building, where Congress meets. It was an impressive building. So large. I knew J.C. was famous, but I never really understood the power of his fame until that day in D.C. I knew then and there that I wanted to be like J.C. I wanted to know important people. I wanted to be successful. I caught the bug at age twelve.

We spent the last night in J.C.'s RV, which was fun. J.C. made popcorn and we watched one of J.C.'s favorite movies, *Monty Python and the Holy Grail*, on the TV with the VCR. When

I woke around eight in the morning we were more than halfway home. J.C. got an early start and let me sleep. My head was still spinning when we pulled into J.C.'s driveway. J.C. just rocked it that weekend. I was in awe of him.

CHAPTER TWENTY-TWO

REMEMBERING NAMES

"**O**ne of the things that everyone shares in common, rich or poor, is their inability to remember names of people they meet infrequently. It's embarrassing to forget someone's name, and even worse when they remember your name. Making the effort to remember someone's name tells them that they are important to you. Since everyone thinks they are the most important person in the world, and they are, when we forget their names it's a slap in their face. It says you don't care about them, and when we think someone doesn't care about us, we don't care about them either. If you want to build strong, valuable relationships, you have to remember names.

Successful, wealthy people make an effort to compensate for this human failing by utilizing certain tricks to help them remember names. One trick I found very effective is the grouping strategy. With the grouping strategy, you categorize each one of your relationships into a specific group. For example, if you play tennis, you may meet many individuals from various tennis teams or clubs. You may not see these people regularly and, therefore, you forget their names. So you group these infrequent tennis contacts into your tennis group category. Keep a notebook by your side, at all times, with all of your contacts grouped by category. Just prior to getting together with your tennis group, you simply whip out your notebook and review all those listed under the tennis group category. Here are the steps for creating your own specific groups:

Step #1: Write down the name of a new introduction immediately after the introduction. I keep a small pad and pen with me at all times just for this purpose. When your dad was in high school I would go to his volleyball games. I would always run into parents of other kids on your dad's team. I would introduce myself and they would tell me their name. When they weren't looking, I'd pull out my little notepad and write down their name under the letters 'VB' along with some physical description so I could remember them. The next time I'd see them at a game I would walk right up to them and say 'hey John' or "hey Sue.' Most of the time they wouldn't remember my name and I could tell they were a little embarrassed. The interesting thing is that as the volleyball season went on, those same embarrassed parents made sure they got to know my name. I was probably one of the few parents whose name they knew.

Step #2: Associate their face with someone you know or some outstanding facial feature and write this association down in your pad. For example, 'looks like John McEnroe.'

Step #3: Create group categories for all of your contacts, and then assign each contact to a group category. Keep it simple. Not too many groups.

Step #4: Refer to your grouping category just prior to getting together with that group.

This grouping strategy works great. People are amazed by my memory, and I often receive compliments. I usually respond to these compliments by telling that person that I remember the names of people I like. Their chest swells and their egos get stroked. More importantly, they won't ever forget my name."

CHAPTER TWENTY-THREE

THE ONE-HOUR RULE

Another rainy day forced us back indoors to J.C.'s gym. As I stepped on the treadmill, J.C. jumped on his StairMaster contraption and the lesson began.

"This will be another short, but important, lesson," J.C. said as he adjusted the setting on his StairMaster. "It's called the one-hour rule."

As soon as J.C. started exercising, he started teaching.

"Wealthy, successful people do not make a habit of watching TV. If they do watch TV, they watch less than an hour a day or they watch something educational, historical, or informative. Successful people understand that watching recreational TV is a waste of time. Instead, they spend their time engaged in self-improvement activities, participating in nonprofit groups, going to school, teaching, writing, speaking, or reading. Basically, a lot of the rich habits things we've been talking about. Recreational TV is a poverty habit that holds you back in life and contributes to individual poverty. You want to avoid it like the plague. You need to make a habit of limiting time wasters during the day. The one-hour rule helps you do that. The one-hour rule is a habit parents need to teach their kids. They need to teach their kids by their words and actions that spending more than an hour a day watching TV or engaging in similar time wasters is not allowed. It takes away from productive activities like reading or studying. Kids are always watching their parents. If they see their parents sitting in front of the TV, they will do the same. Parents need to lead by example. They need to not only monitor their kids and make sure they are not spending more than an hour a day on TV or engaged in similar time-wasting activities; they need to also limit their consumption of TV and time wasters to no more than an hour a day. It needs to become a household rule that everyone follows.

Kids who learn the one-hour rule get better grades in school, and when they become adults this translates into better paying jobs, with bigger raises and larger bonuses during their working career. As a consequence, they accumulate more wealth in life. Parents who don't teach their kids the one-hour rule are missing out on an important success-mentoring opportunity. By following this one-hour rule, kids will have more time to read, exercise, and join groups that will help them develop more relationships in life. Parents need to be the ones who require that their kids read for education or self-help at least thirty minutes each day. The reality is, most kids won't develop the daily habit of reading for self-improvement on their own. They develop the daily habit of reading for self-improvement when their parents make it become a habit. Parents also need to teach their kids the daily habit of exercising aerobically twenty to thirty minutes a day. That's running, jogging, biking, etc. Wealthy people are healthy people. Being healthy for your entire life will mean fewer sick days, more energy, more productivity, aaannnddd . . ."

J.C. hung on to that last word. I thought he was waiting for me to fill in the blank, so I did.

"And happiness and success in life?"

J.C. was so excited he nearly fell of the StairMaster. I started to laugh. He was like a little kid opening his gifts at Christmas.

"Yep, more happiness and success." J.C. clapped his hands together. "Hey, you're catching on. We're going to talk more about health tomorrow."

I turned to Brendan in the car. "We now have the Internet, cell phones, and all sorts of other electronic devices. Those things are replacing the TV. That same one-hour rule applies to all those things," I told Brendan. "Wasting time on your cell phone and the Internet is just as bad as wasting time watching TV," I said.

CHAPTER TWENTY-FOUR
WEALTHY PEOPLE ARE HEALTHY PEOPLE

"**W**ealthy, successful people eat right and exercise every day. They watch not only what they eat, but also how much they eat. They manage their consumption of food. As a rule, successful people do not binge or overindulge in food or drink. If they do slip, it is managed overindulgence, relegated to that of an infrequent occurrence, such as a holiday meal or a party, rather than a regular occurrence. Eating right helps keep the pounds off. Seventy percent of all weight loss comes from eating less. Eating right also reduces the risk of heart disease by reducing your cholesterol level. Good cholesterol is called HDL. Bad cholesterol is called LDL. Your overall cholesterol level should be about three times your HDL. As a rule, you want your total cholesterol level below 180.

Good cholesterol foods include alcohol in moderation, artichokes, avocados, baked potatoes, beans, berries, bran muffins, chicken, dark chocolate, eggs, high fiber foods, fruits, vegetables, garlic, green tea, niacin, nuts (especially walnuts), oatmeal, olive oil, omega-3 fat supplements, onions, orange juice, popcorn, raisins, salmon, halibut, mackerel, trout, tuna, soy products, tomatoes, turkey, and whole grain pasta. All of these foods are high in HDL cholesterol.

There are a lot of bad cholesterol foods. Hold on, this is a long list: bacon, bologna, butter, cakes, cheese, clams, coconuts, cookies, crackers, doughnuts, egg yolk, french fries, fried foods in general, ham, hamburger, hot dogs, ice cream, lamb chops, mashed potatoes, mayonnaise, milk, movie theater popcorn, onion rings, oysters, pastries, pies, pizza, pork, pot roast, potato chips, red meat, sausage, scallops, lobster, crabs, shrimp, sour cream, steak, sugar, white bread, and yogurt. All of these foods are high in LDL cholesterol.

For successful people, exercise is a routine, like brushing their teeth. They understand that daily exercise improves their bodies and minds. Routine aerobic exercise improves the immune system and results in fewer sick days. This increases productivity, since the frequency of sick days, for those who exercise aerobically, is less than that of others. People who regularly exercise also have more energy during the day.

Successful people have a system, or routine, for weight management that works best for them. Some have sophisticated systems, some less sophisticated, but most 'manage' their weight.

Unsuccessful people have no consistent, day-to-day control over their health. They are always in search of the latest and greatest quick-fix diet idea. Unsuccessful people deal with health matters sporadically and usually require outside influences to motivate them to eat less or eat differently. This is the reason why there are so many diet books out there. With little control over their eating habits, they go through phases of gaining and losing weight again and again. This behavior takes a toll on the body, which eventually manifests as medical problems, such as high blood pressure, diabetes, heart disease, stuff like that.

Unsuccessful people approach exercise the same way they approach their consumption of food, requiring some outside force to momentarily motivate them. When that motivation wears off, they fall back into bad habits, stop exercising, and gain weight as part of a cycle that recurs throughout their lives.

In beginning a weight-management program, you need to first gain an understanding of the specific foods you eat on a daily basis. During the first thirty days of your weight management program you'll need to track what you normally eat and figure out the number of calories for each food item. During this thirty-day period, you'll be able to identify certain foods that are high in calories, and this allows you to know which high-calorie foods to avoid.

Never confuse managing what you eat with dieting. They are not the same. Diets don't work in managing weight in the long term. The reason is that they are too restrictive and, quite frankly, they take the fun out of life. Managing what you eat does not mean starving or never eating junk food. Trust me, you're going to eat junk food. The trick is to keep it to three hundred junk food calories a day. You simply need to understand that you can't eat high-calorie foods every day, as this will push you over your daily caloric threshold, which is the threshold you need to stay within in order to lose or maintain your weight. You should feel free to eat and drink the things you like when the spirit moves you. But you need to understand that eating some of the foods you love might mean occasionally exceeding your caloric threshold for that day, which is fine as long as this is the exception and not the rule.

Monitoring food consumption only gets you halfway toward managing weight. You must engage in a daily aerobic exercise regimen for at least twenty to thirty minutes a day, four days per week. Jogging outdoors provides the most effective results. The number of calories burned with jogging is greater by about one-third than an indoor treadmill, StairMaster, or stationary bike. Lifting weights, sit-ups, push-ups, and the like are good supplements to any basic aerobic activity, but they are not substitutes for aerobic activity. By themselves, these exercises will not help you lose weight as much as they will help you shape and tone your body. Aerobic activity is the most reliable activity to help you lose weight and should be the foundation for your exercise regimen.

For most, morning is the best time to do your daily exercise. It all depends on your job. Some people work at night so their 'mornings' might be 5 p.m. If you do your exercising before your work day begins, you're less likely to be pulled away by scheduling issues or conflicts that often occur during the day.

A great tool to monitor your weight is my tracking schedule. Tracking takes only five minutes each day. You will begin to see patterns in your weight management that enable you to better understand your body and allow you to gain control over your weight. Within two months of completing my tracking schedule, you will be able to determine your individual daily caloric threshold, and you can then manage your calorie intake to lose or maintain your weight. For example, assume your daily caloric threshold is 2,100 calories per day, given the level of exercise you do. If you consume less than 2,100 calories each day, you will lose weight every day. If you consume more than 2,100 calories each day, you will gain weight, every day. I'll give you a copy of the tracking schedule when we get back to the house."

When we got back to the house J.C. and I walked over to his office to get that tracking schedule you see in the notebook.

TRACKING SCHEDULE

BEG. WEIGHT	
GOAL WEIGHT	
END WEIGHT	
GOAL CALORIES PER DAY	

DATE	WEIGHT	AEROBIC EXERCISE	SPORTS ACTIVITIES	BREAKFAST CALORIES	LUNCH CALORIES	DINNER CALORIES	TOTAL CALORIES	CUMULATIVE CALORIES	AVERAGE CALORIES

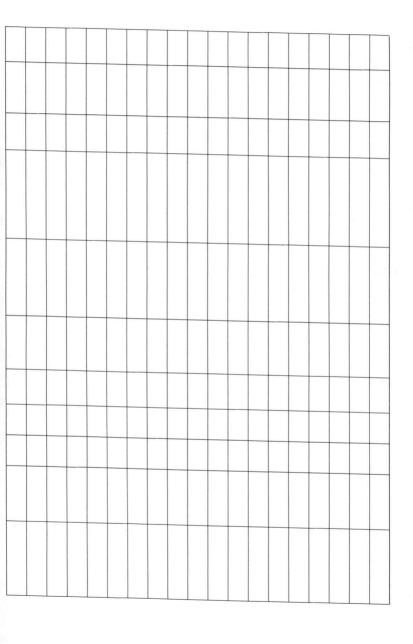

MONTH	AEROBIC EXERCISE DAYS	MINUTES	MILES	AVGERAGE CALORIES	LBS (LOST)/ GAINED	BEG WEIGHT	END WEIGHT			
JANUARY										
FEBRUARY										
MARCH										
APRIL										
MAY										
JUNE										
JULY										
AUGUST										
SEPTEMBER										
OCTOBER										
NOVEMBER										
DECEMBER										

CHAPTER TWENTY-FIVE

PROCRASTINATION

"It's the little things, done every day, that create success in life. Fear holds you back from doing what you need to do and is a major cause of procrastination. Fear is also a negative emotion, and negative emotions attract poverty and, thus, prevent you from becoming financially successful in life. Making a habit of overcoming procrastination is a rich habit that will put an end to this costly negative emotion and will attract wealth into your life.

Wealthy, successful people believe they are in control of their lives and their circumstances. They do not let life, circumstances, or events control them. As a result, they are responsive to clients, patients, business partners, family, and friends. Successful people are goal oriented. They set goals and achieve them. They are constantly completing tasks and projects in a timely manner. They are proactive. Consequently, they are not engaged in the practice of putting out fires or dealing with emergencies. They ignore the voice of procrastination.

Unsuccessful people procrastinate. They delay, put off, and defer things that should and could be done that very day. Their procrastination creates problems that require immediate attention. It increases the risk of forgetting something important, or dealing with a critical matter in an emergency setting, which risks mistakes, errors, and legal liabilities that can result in lawsuits. Procrastination leads to poor quality in whatever service they provide. The lives of unsuccessful people are haphazard, confused, and complicated. They don't accomplish much, as they are constantly putting out one fire after another. They react, instead, to outside forces, which command their immediate attention. They have no control over their lives or their daily schedules. They feel powerless and directionless."

J.C. then went over the four strategies successful people use to eliminate procrastination:

"STRATEGY #1 TO-DO LISTS

Successful people use to-do lists to get things done. To-do lists are like daily goals. There are two types of daily to-dos:

Goal To-Dos — These are daily tasks tied to monthly, yearly, and long-term goals. These are almost always fixed in nature, meaning the same to-dos show up every day on the to-do list. For example: "Make ten telemarketing phone calls.

Non-Goal To-Dos — These are to-dos that are unrelated to any goals. They may be administrative tasks, client tasks, or daily obligations. They may be fixed, daily tasks or they may vary daily."

When we got back home we went over to his office and he gave me the to-do list chart you see there in the notebook:

TO DO LIST

TIME

DESCRIPTION	MONDAY	TUESDAY	WEDNESDAY	THURSDAY	FRIDAY
Self-Improvement reading	5AM-5:30AM	5AM-5:30AM	5AM-5:30AM	5AM-5:30AM	5AM-5:30AM
Exercise	5:30AM-6AM	5:30AM-6AM	5:30AM-6AM	5:30AM-6AM	5:30AM-6AM
Prepare To-Do list	6AM-6:30AM	6AM-6:30AM	6AM-6:30AM	6AM-6:30AM	6AM-6:30AM
Make 10 telemarketing calls	9AM-10AM	9AM-10AM	9AM-10AM	9AM-10AM	9AM-10AM
Work on client projection	10AM-12PM				
Work on client business plan		10AM-12PM			
Work on client marketing project			10AM-12PM		
Work on client tax provision				10AM-12PM	
Networking lunch meeting	12:30-2PM	12:30-2PM	12:30-2PM	12:30-2PM	12:30-2PM
Return all calls	2:30-3:30PM	2:30-3:30PM	2:30-3:30PM	2:30-3:30PM	2:30-3:30PM
Client projects	3:30-6PM	3:30-6PM	3:30-6PM	3:30-6PM	3:30-6PM

"STRATEGY #2 DAILY FIVE

Many of the millionaires in my study adopted processes that helped them make more money and accumulate large amounts of wealth. One such process is the daily five. The daily five is a strategy that will help you accomplish your goals. On a piece of paper, list every conceivable activity that will help you move closer to your goals. Then process these activities into your day. Every day, attack your major goals by engaging in at least five activities. It may not seem like you are accomplishing a lot but, over time, these small daily accomplishments add up and will move you closer to achieving your overall goals. Each day, check off the five things you accomplished, and continue doing this day in and day out. You will be amazed how quickly this daily five strategy will help you accomplish all of your major goals in life.

STRATEGY #3 'DO IT NOW' AFFIRMATIONS

When the thought of putting something off enters your mind, immediately cast this thought out by saying, 'Do it now.' Repeat these three words a hundred times a day if you have to. Don't allow thoughts of procrastination even a second of life. Once you are fully engaged in an activity, you will soon find yourself absorbed in the activity, and all thoughts of procrastinating will be gone.

STRATEGY #4 SETTING DEADLINES

Setting deadlines for accomplishing daily goals or items on your to-do list creates an itch in your brain that can only be scratched by completing tasks and meeting the self-imposed deadline. The itch is an unrelenting guilt that will not go away until you accomplish the task."

CHAPTER TWENTY-SIX

VOLUNTEERING

J.C. gave me a little history lesson on volunteering before getting into the meat of the lesson.

"The roots of volunteerism in America go back very far. Benjamin Franklin was perhaps one of the most prodigious volunteers in our nation's history, having organized the Philadelphia volunteer fire company, a militia, circulating libraries, public hospitals, mutual insurance companies, and agricultural colleges, as well as intellectual societies. He was also, not coincidentally, the most famous American in the world during his day, admired by millions around the world.

Wealthy, successful people make a habit of volunteering. They volunteer five or more hours each month. When you volunteer in your community you gain name recognition. It exposes you to more people and expands your relationship base. You become a recognized figure in your community, and that makes you feel important. There is no better feeling than the feeling that you made a difference. I like to call it the 'George Bailey effect.' George Bailey is the name of the main character in that movie *It's a Wonderful Life*. We watch it together on Christmas Day. Anyway, the point is, we all want to feel our lives have meaning. Volunteering satisfies that empty feeling we sometimes have about our very existence. When our volunteerism makes a difference, it simply makes us feel like we matter in life.

Volunteering allows you to meet new people and gain new relationships. These relationships can turn into life-long friendships or business acquaintances. If you have had difficulty making new relationships, volunteering may be the perfect remedy.

Volunteering is a perfect way to highlight your skill set. When you do a good job, people notice, and that very often translates into business or job opportunities. People want to do business with people they know, like, and trust. What better way to make that happen than volunteering?"

When we finished reviewing our final lesson of the week, J.C. clapped his hands together.

"OK. What time is everyone getting here?"

I looked at J.C. with an excitement that penetrated deep into my bones. "A few hours. They said they'd be here around lunchtime."

"Got your stuff all packed?" J.C. asked.

"I was packed on Monday."

J.C. laughed. "Great. Let's load the RV and get some rest. We're gonna need it."

CHAPTER TWENTY-SEVEN
THE WORLD'S GREATEST HAMBURGER

We loaded our bags into the storage area underneath the RV, and then headed to our rooms to catch a few hours of shut-eye before my friends arrived. This was going to be a trip of a lifetime for everyone. We were taking the RV for an eight-day trip to New Orleans, Louisiana, to a place J.C. said made the best hamburgers in the world. J.C. would know. He'd been on every continent. He dined with presidents, kings, premiers, emperors, you name it. When J.C. said we were going to a place that served the world's greatest hamburger, I had no doubt in my mind he knew what he was talking about. J.C.'s description of New Orleans, or NOLA, as he liked to call it, was of a magical place, filled with music, people dancing, exotic food, and excitement at every turn. Jazz was a big deal in NOLA, J.C. said. J.C. called NOLA the only true melting pot in America, because he said it was the only place where different cultures melded into one unique culture. J.C.'s tales of NOLA danced inside my mind and followed me as I drifted off to sleep.

Like clockwork, cars, filled with my best friends, began arriving at noon. J.C. was in the back cooking up hot dogs and chicken wings. We all stuffed ourselves while J.C. and the parents packed the RV with backpacks, suitcases, tents, and coolers.

"Five minutes. Brush your teeth, hit the john, and be in the RV in five minutes," J.C. bellowed from the porch.

We all scrambled up the stairs and battled ferociously for bathrooms. We flew down the stairs and into the RV, settling in for our trip to NOLA to sample the finest hamburger cuisine known to man. The excitement of Christmas morning paled in comparison.

We were on the road at 1 p.m. and didn't stop until we reached our first campgrounds at Shenandoah National Park in the Blue Ridge Mountains of western Virginia. We spent the night camping outside the RV and woke at daybreak. After breakfast, we helped J.C. unload the fishing and hiking gear. Shenandoah National Park has over 500 miles of trails, including 101 miles of the Appalachian Trail. Some trails led to waterfalls that faded away into rivers and streams perfect for fishing. We threw our fishing poles into the banks of the Rose River to hunt for fish.

After a few hours of fishing, J.C. took us on a short hike to a nearby watering hole with a long, thick rope that would launch you high into the air, allowing gravity to pull you down into the water with a big splash. We stripped down to our bathing suits as fast as we could and took turns flying into the air like trapeze artists. The water was cold, but we couldn't give a crap. It was the closest thing to paradise on earth.

After our water acrobatics, we headed back to the RV for some lunch and to resume our journey to find the world's greatest hamburger. Our next stop would be Great Smoky Mountains National Park. The Great Smoky Mountains are a mountain range rising along the Tennessee– North Carolina border. When we arrived and had finished setting up our campsite, we headed over to Cades Cove. J.C. went inside a building and a few minutes later we were all on horseback following behind a guide who took us on a horse trail around Cades Cove. None of us had ever been on a horse before, so we were all a little afraid at first, but that fear soon faded away into a rush of adrenaline. The guide gave all of us a history lesson on the geology and wildlife of the park and took us around creeks and some old buildings that were called gristmills. A gristmill is a place where you can grind grain into flour. Gristmills were a very important part of the community in the old pioneering days of America. Farmers would bring in their grain to grind, in return for a fee from the miller. Millers often took their fees in trade, selling or trading grain and flour with other villagers in exchange for stuff that people needed in those days to survive, like livestock, vegetables, and tools.

When we were done with our horseback ride, we headed back to camp, had some lunch, and began our last leg of the journey to our final stop—NOLA. J.C. did a good job fueling our anticipation during the drive. The anticipation of seeing all the sights of NOLA and eating the world's greatest hamburger stayed with us for the entire trip.

We arrived on the outskirts of NOLA sometime around one in the morning. We were all still wide awake. J.C. pulled into a hotel parking lot, parked the RV, and directed us inside. We spent the rest of that short night in the largest suite in the hotel.

"Get some sleep. You're gonna need it. We've got a lot to do tomorrow," J.C. commanded.

Excitement soon gave way to exhaustion, and after a short while we were all fast asleep, dreaming about NOLA and the adventure that awaited us at daybreak.

Our first stop was breakfast at a famous spot called Cafe du Monde on the banks of the Mississippi River in the New Orleans French Market. J.C. ordered all of us something called beignets. Beignets are square shaped doughnuts, covered with powdered sugar. Some of the beignets were filled with bananas, others with strawberries, and others had no fruit at all. They were delicious.

After sampling the beignets, we headed up the stairs behind Cafe du Monde for a steamboat ride along the Mississippi River. Just after we settled down at our table, this loud steam whistle went off, and then the boat started to move. Breakfast included all this food I had never heard of before. There was soup called gumbo, something called shrimp etouffee, jambalaya, red beans and rice, and the most delicious dessert I had ever had called bananas fosters.

J.C. only let us sample the food. "Don't eat too much, boys. The world's greatest hamburger awaits us."

As we ate, a jazz band began to play. After our light meal, we headed to the top deck, which had this incredible view of the river. Everyone on the boat was so friendly and pleasant. The two-hour ride seemed to last but a few minutes. What an experience.

After the steamboat ride, J.C. took us on a tour of the French Quarter. He explained that NOLA's unique culture was actually the melding together of six distinct cultures: Spanish, French, Creole, African, Native American Indian, and original American settlers. One of my friends asked what Creole was and J.C. gave us a history lesson.

"Many Americans like to say our nation is a melting pot of different cultures, but the reality is that most of America is a patchwork of cultures, not a melting pot. You have some areas that are German ancestry, some that are Irish, Italian, Greek, etc. Except in NOLA. In NOLA they have Creole. Creole people are descended from the colonial settlers in Louisiana. They're a combination of French, Spanish, and Africans, primarily from the Caribbean. Creoles are not one thing, they are everything—black, white, French, Spanish, with some Native American Indian thrown in there. They embody what it means to be an American. They are truly a melting pot. When they talk about America being a melting pot, they are talking about NOLA."

When we finished our two-hour tour, J.C. clapped his hands together and, with a loud roar, announced, "It's hamburger time!"

We all boarded something called a streetcar, which was a green trolley that ran all over NOLA. NOLA was famous for its streetcars. J.C. said NOLA had the oldest continuously operating streetcars in the world. The one we were on ran between and underneath these old cypress trees, another thing NOLA was famous for. The world's greatest hamburger was a long walk from where the streetcar dropped us off, but we didn't mind. It was a beautiful day, with the sun shining through those magnificent cypress trees. The trees had this stuff hanging down from the branches that J.C. said was Spanish moss. It looked like the trees actually had long hair growing from their branches.

At the end of our journey, J.C. announced, "There it is."

We stood outside a small restaurant called Port of Call. There was a long line of people waiting to get inside.

"Stay here. Don't move. I'll be right out," J.C. said. He made his way through the throng of people waiting to get inside and after a few minutes we saw his head pop out from the door, waving us in.

J.C. never had to wait in lines. He knew everyone. Evidently, the family who owned Port of Call were close friends with J.C. and a famous chef from NOLA, who was one of J.C.'s best friends in NOLA. So we were ushered inside, past all the people waiting in line. We felt like royalty. They had a table already set up in the back for our arrival. Everyone ordered hamburgers. They were huge. And delicious. J.C. was spot on. They were the best hamburgers any of us had ever had. If I had two stomachs I would have ordered two hamburgers, even though I could hardly finish the one I had. It practically covered the entire plate.

We walked back to the streetcar stop, hopped on the streetcar, and headed back to the French Quarter and our hotel.

"You've got three hours to do as you please," J.C. bellowed as soon as we stepped inside our suite.

The hotel had a pool, so my friends and I headed down to the pool and spent the next few hours there.

When we eventually made our way back to the suite, J.C. told us we had an hour to get ready.

"A friend of mine is going to make us dinner."

J.C. arranged a few cabs to take us to a restaurant called the Commander's Palace in the Garden District. When we arrived, they sat us at a table in the back, by the kitchen. After a few minutes this real Italian-looking guy came out from the kitchen, dressed to the nines in this impressive white chef outfit. J.C. stood up immediately and let out a loud "*bam.*" The chef guy laughed, ran over to J.C., shook his hand, and then gave him a big bear hug.

"Kids, I'd like to introduce you to the greatest chef in the world, Emeril Lagasse." Emeril went around the table and introduced himself, then ran into the kitchen and came out with seven cookbooks. He signed his name to each and gave each of us a copy. He was so energetic, like a chef on steroids.

"Boys, have I got a meal for you," Emeril said and then explained, in incredible detail, what he had cooked up for us that night. By the time dinner began to arrive we were all salivating. The meal was delicious. Everything NOLA, finished off with all sorts of desserts, including my new favorite, bananas fosters. When we were done, we could hardly lift ourselves from our seats.

We headed back to the Jersey Shore early the following morning filled with memories about our trip that would stay with us forever. Once again, J.C. did it. He exceeded our wildest expectations. He always seemed to do that. That was just J.C.

CHAPTER TWENTY-EIGHT
RICH THINKING

J.C. said this lesson, like some of the other lessons, was going to be a little long and that he needed me to stay focused, as he was going to move a little quicker than usual.

"Wealthy, successful people are positive thinkers. They feel powerful, in control, confident, and energized. This is not by accident. They are disciples of rich thinking. Rich thinking attracts success and happiness. The foundation of rich thinking is positive thinking. Successful people use certain strategies to help them stay positive and avoid negative thinking.

1. **Daily Affirmations**

2. **Visualizations**

3. **Goal Setting**

4. **The Victory Log**

5. **Future Mirror Strategies**

We covered most of these already except the victory log and the future mirror strategies, which we'll cover soon enough. What I want to cover today about rich thinking is how the brain works. We really have multiple brains. The two main parts are the conscious and the subconscious. Both drive our behaviors in life. The conscious is willed behavior. Stuff we can control at will. The subconscious is habitual or automatic behavior. Stuff that's outside our control. Our behavior is the product of perceptions, feelings, and thoughts. Some are conscious behaviors and some are subconscious behaviors. Remember when we talked about rich habits and poverty habits and how both are stored in the basal ganglia? That basal ganglia is part of the subconscious, so our habits are part of the subconscious. Sigmund Freud was a famous neurologist who made a living talking about how the subconscious was responsible for many of our perceptions, emotions, and behavior. Thanks to Freud, the study of the subconscious became a big deal. He pointed out that a lot of the decisions we make in life are directed by our subconscious. Our thoughts, followed by our actions, dictate our circumstances in life. It's all about cause and effect. If our thinking is positive, it will be followed by actions that are directed by our positive thinking. This is the source of wealth: rich thinking followed by rich habits. If our thinking is negative, it will be followed by actions that are directed by our negative thinking. Poverty thinking is the source of poverty: poverty thinking followed by poverty habits. Generally, rich thinking and poverty thinking are learned from our parents or some mentor in life.

If your thoughts and emotions are anchored in positive thinking, your subconscious will work to your advantage. It will help direct your behavior in a positive way. The way the subconscious talks to us is through something called intuition. Intuition is the little voice in your head that tells you what to do or what not to do. When you're in a positive thinking mindset, intuition works.

For example, if you are grateful for the money you make, no matter how large or small it may be, your subconscious will say things to you that will be in line with your positive thinking and help bring you more money. Being grateful for any money you receive says to your subconscious that you like having money. Your subconscious gets the message and then it goes to work to alter your behavior so you can get more money. It will motivate you to do things, or not do things, in an effort to cause more money to flow to you.

If your thoughts and emotions are anchored in negative thinking, however, your subconscious will work against you. Your intuition won't work to help you. It will actually work against you by telling you to do things that are consistent with your negative thinking. For example, if you're constantly telling yourself you don't have enough money, your intuition will accept that as a belief and tell you to do things that will make sure you always don't have enough money. It will keep you poor. It will direct your behavior to keep you poor. It's not an accident that most people in the world are poor. Most of them are drowning in negative thinking, and that voice in their head is working against them, keeping them poor. It's not entirely their fault. From the time we are learning to walk, we are bombarded with negative programming from our parents. Our early lives were filled with 'no's' and 'don'ts' and 'cant's' and all sorts of negative programming. 'No, you can't have that toy; we don't have the money.' 'Don't play with matches; you'll get burned.' 'We can't go to Disney like Ryan's family, because they're rich and we're not.' 'Look both ways before crossing the street or you'll get hit by a car.' 'Eat your food, there are people in Africa starving right now.'

All this negative programming fills us with worry, doubt, anxiety, jealousy, and envy. We grow up to be fearful and ungrateful. And it stays with most of us for our entire lives, embedded deep in our subconscious mind, guiding us, directing us, controlling us. We become adults filled with fear. We avoid risk and change. We envy what others have. This is most of us. This is also the poor. All this negativity, this fear and ungratefulness, are like mini computer programs that have been fed into our subconscious mind. The subconscious then goes about looking for ways to help us get more of the negative things we constantly think about. It starts whispering in our ears, advising us, guiding us, in an effort to give us more of what we think about and believe. When we are in a negative, ungrateful state, that voice inside our head, our intuition, is telling us to do things that will keep us poor, worried, and jealous of others. It is directing us toward unhappiness and failure. For most, intuition simply does not work to improve our lives, and we should ignore that voice inside our head.

In order to get the voice inside our head working properly, directing us towards happiness and success, we need to shift to a positive, grateful, and optimistic mindset. Start by making a point to find something to be grateful for each day. Focus on that thing we are grateful for and try to feel the gratitude. Feelings and emotions lock it in. If we can't feel it, our subconscious will not get that line of computer code. Once we feel the gratitude, it's like laying railroad tracks inside our brain. When we live in a grateful, optimistic, positive mental world, the subconscious looks for ways to help us get more of what we are thinking about. It starts to whisper things in our ears that are directing us toward happiness and success. Then it's time to listen. We'll talk more about emotions in the next lesson. It's a big subject. It may take a few days to get through."

CHAPTER TWENTY-NINE

RICH EMOTIONS

"Rich emotions are positive emotions. Those who are wealthy and successful understand that rich emotions create wealth and success. Rich emotions attract into your life good things. Poverty emotions attract into your life bad things. We'll get into poverty emotions tomorrow.

The very starting point of success is to change your thinking from negative to positive. You do this by controlling your emotions. Our emotions reside in the subconscious. The subconscious only receives thoughts created from our conscious mind when those thoughts are accompanied by an emotion. Emotions are the key to opening the door between the subconscious mind and the conscious mind. Why is it important for the subconscious mind to receive a thought from the conscious mind? It's important because the subconscious mind can turn any emotionalized thought it receives into reality. If you want to become rich and successful, you need to feed your subconscious mind with an emotionalized thought so that it may go to work and make you rich and successful. It does that by feeding your conscious mind with subconscious thoughts, called intuition, which alter your behavior. If your emotionalized thoughts are positive-type thoughts, the subconscious then goes to work, behind the scenes, to bring about success in your life. Thoughts that bring about success must be positive thoughts anchored to rich emotions. If your emotionalized thoughts are negative-type thoughts, the subconscious then goes to work, behind the scenes, to bring about failure in your life."

J.C. then rattled off the top ten rich emotions you see in my notebook:

1. Love

2. Gratitude

3. Happiness

4. Belief

5. Courage

6. Confidence

7. Enthusiasm

8. Forgiveness

9. Amusement

10. Peace

"Love is the most powerful emotion. Love makes us do things that we would never otherwise do. We will go to any lengths to protect and help those we love. Love alters our behavior. Using the daily five strategy we talked about the other day, make a daily list of five people you love and every day say 'I love you' to yourself for each one of them. Feel the love deep in your bones. To help emotionalize it, think about a person on your list, and try to remember something you did with that person that was so much fun and made you happy. That triggers the love emotion.

Gratitude is another powerful rich emotion. When we make a daily habit out of being grateful, our subconscious interprets this to mean we want more things to be grateful about. This becomes a directive, and like a guided missile, the subconscious begins the process of attracting more things into our lives for us to be grateful about: more money, more stuff, better relationships, more clients, more sales, more good health, etc. Using the daily five strategy again, make a list of five things you are grateful for every day. To trigger the gratitude emotion, think about anything you received that made you happy.

Human beings are all after one thing—happiness. We all strive to be happy. Every single one of us, without exception. The desire for happiness has been hardwired into our subconscious since the beginning of time. Why? Those who are happy are healthier; their immune systems are stronger, and they are better able to fight off cancer, disease, and infections. Those who are happy have better relationships. They have loving, caring families and friends who desire to spend time with one another every chance they get. Those who are happy make more money. Happiness motivates and drives us. It shows up on the job in the form of better quality, more creative problem solving, and, once again, stronger relationships. The desire to be happy makes humans do some incredible things, such as Mother Teresa's efforts to help the world's poor.

Belief is the antidote for fear and doubt, two poverty emotions. Believing in yourself and in your main purpose in life will eliminate all fears and help you overcome all obstacles life throws in your way. Belief is like a lawn mower. It cuts down and removes all negative emotions that get in the way of pursuing your dreams. The good news is that belief can become a daily habit. Through the use of meditation, visualizations, affirmations, and the future mirror strategy, which I touched on yesterday, you can condition your mind to overcome all fears.

Never question or doubt the workings of the subconscious. That part of the brain is still little understood. One day we will learn more about the subconscious and it won't be so mysterious. For now, just know this: emotionalized thoughts of any kind somehow get into the subconscious and act like a computer program, directing our subconscious to do whatever the emotionalized thought tells it to do. If you're jealous, it gives you more things to be jealous of. If you're grateful, it gives you more things to be grateful for. The formula is really very simple: Gratitude = More Stuff; Envy = Less Stuff.

I created this tool I call the daily mind routine that helps keep you thinking positively, J.C. said and then paused for a moment. We'll tackle that another day."

CHAPTER THIRTY

POVERTY EMOTIONS

"Poverty emotions are negative emotions. When we experience a poverty emotion and allow that emotion to stay with us for more than a few seconds, we are sending a directive to our subconscious. Our subconscious thinks we want it to create negative things in our lives so, like a guided missile, it seeks to attract things into our lives that will perpetuate those poverty emotions."

J.C. then rattled off a list of the poverty emotions you see in the notebook:

- **Hatred**

- **Envy**

- **Sadness**

- **Hopelessness**

- **Fear**

- **Doubt**

- **Apathy**

- **Revenge**

- **Anger**

Hatred is a negative emotion. It is the opposite of love. You must never allow hatred to root itself in your subconscious. It is like a cancer to success. It attracts events and circumstances into your life that are destructive. While happiness is what we all seek for ourselves and our children, hatred gives us the opposite: unhappiness. It leads to excessive drinking, drug use, stress, broken or strained relationships, struggling businesses, and financial difficulties. Never, ever hate if you desire to be wealthy and happy. Replace any thoughts of hatred with love.

From a financial standpoint, envy is the worst of all of the negative emotions. When we are envious we send a message, infused with emotion, to our subconscious, that we lack. The subconscious picks up only the emotionalized thought of not having enough in life. It interprets this negative emotionalized thought of lacking as a directive. When we allow thoughts of envy to enter our minds, we are essentially telling our subconscious to go out and get us more things to be envious of. The law of attraction kicks in and we begin to attract into our lives less income, fewer possessions, more expenses, more debt, etc. The subconscious is only doing what it is programmed to do.

Everyone feels afraid at some point. Any change, even positive changes like marriage or a promotion, can prompt feelings of fear. Wealthy people have conditioned their minds to overcome fear, while poor people give in to fear and allow it to hold them back in life.

There are eight core fears:

- **The fear of failure.**

- **The fear of success.**

- **The fear of rejection.**

- **The fear of not being good enough.**

- **The fear of scarcity.**

- **The fear of being alone.**

- **The fear of losing control.**

- **The fear of being different or standing out.**

Sadness is the opposite of happiness. Sadness weakens our immune system and our overall health. Sadness destroys relationships. People go out of their way to avoid sad people. Those who are sad make less money because they have little to no drive. Their productivity suffers and the quality of their work product suffers. They lose the ability to create: a fundamental human trait. They accomplish very little in life because they are despondent and listless."

"One last thing about sadness," J.C. said, with his hands locked behind his back and his head pointed down at the boardwalk.

"Looking into the past attracts sadness. Avoid the habit of reminiscing about the past and create the habit of feeling hopeful about the future. This is another reason why goals are so important. Goals act like a shield against sadness.

Doubt is the opposite of faith, belief, and confidence. It is one of the most common of the negative emotions. Doubt puts the brakes on goal achievement. It creates indecision. Doubt is part of the poverty thinking that holds most back in life and is one of the reasons why there are so many living paycheck to paycheck. Doubt holds people back from taking risks in life. When you are filled with doubt, you are filled with poverty thinking.

When we allow the revenge emotion into our thoughts, our subconscious takes this as a directive and begins to attract more bad things into our lives in order for us to continue to feel vengeful. More people come into our lives to steal from us, to physically harm us, and to undermine us.

Uncontrolled anger is responsible for many poor decisions and consequences. Some of those decisions and consequences put people behind bars, cause a loss of employment, destroy relationships, hurt families, and jeopardize your health and safety. Controlling anger requires that you make a habit of doing three things: *think . . . evaluate . . .* and *react . . .*"

J.C. seemed to want to pound each word into my brain.

"There are a lot of people in prison today because they didn't follow this simple rule. Thinking forces you to use your mind and not your emotions. Evaluate applies mental logic to buy you time to process the situation. React is the last thing you do after carefully considering and thinking through any important event in life. Reacting to any situation in life should be the very last thing you do. Never react first. It's the kiss of death. This simple formula takes emotion out of the equation and replaces it with logic. This process reverses the order and puts the brain in charge of dealing with complicated situations in life."

CHAPTER THIRTY-ONE

THE DAILY MIND ROUTINE

A s we began to make our way to the boardwalk, J.C. handed me a piece of paper.

"That's my daily mind routine." It was a long list. I looked it over.

1. Meditate for fifteen minutes first thing upon waking up.

2. Read affirmations.

3. Read gratitude list.

4. Say "I love you" with emotion, for those I love.

5. Future mirror letters.

6. Review vision board.

7. Meditate for fifteen minutes right before sleep.

Meditation

- Sit in a chair and get comfortable.

- Close eyes.

- Feel your eyes relax, then your whole head, then your neck, then your shoulders, then your chest, then your arms, then your waist, then your legs, and then your feet.

- Take thirty deep breaths and see each number in your head. Let all thoughts drift by one after the other, like railroad cars on a track.

- Visualize your big dreams coming true. Visualize all of your goals being realized.

- Visualize your ideal life, with your ideal home, your ideal job, your ideal income, and your ideal health. See yourself happy and successful.

- Ask for help in overcoming any obstacles that are in your way.

- Open eyes and say, "I am happy."

Affirmations

J.C.'s list had about twenty affirmations on his list. One stuck out:

- Teach my grandson how to be happy and successful in life this summer.

Gratitude List

J.C. listed all of the things he was grateful for in life. He listed names of family, friends, business associates, all of his rich habits trainers and students, and his house down the shore. This list went on and on for five pages.

One-Year Letter

J.C.'s one-year letter was dated one year into the future. It was a letter to himself about all the things he had accomplished during the year. All the goals he realized, the number of speaking and training engagements he did, the completion of his latest book, and the fun things he did during the previous summer, with his grandson.

Five-Year Letter

This was a lot like J.C.'s one-year letter, except it was dated five years into the future. He had bigger goals in there for himself that he accomplished, stuff he did for the family, how much he was worth. That one caught my eye. "I was able to add another ten million dollars to my wealth."

Vision Board

J.C.'s vision board included pictures of a building on the water by a beautiful beach, with the words "next speaking engagement" underneath, a picture of himself jogging, and another picture of John McEnroe hitting a ball with the words "I play tennis with John McEnroe" written below it. There was another with a large yacht with the words "family vacation" also written below the picture, as well as a few other pictures with J.C.'s words underneath.

After I was done going through J.C.'s list, I looked up toward J.C. J.C. then began to teach.

"I go through that mind routine every day. You want to do your meditation in the morning and at night. Meditation is good programming for the subconscious. The subconscious is most receptive to programming immediately after you wake up in the morning and right before you go to bed. That's when the rich thinking stuff really sinks in. The affirmations are all tied to some goal I want to accomplish. My major goal this summer is to teach you everything I know that can help make you happy and successful in life. Every day I express gratitude for the things I have, my family, my friends, the money I make, the wealth I have. Always be grateful for the smallest things in life as well as the big stuff. Every day I express love for my family, friends, and the various people who made or make this great life of mine possible. Gratitude and love keep your thinking positive. It's easy to allow negative thoughts to dominate your thinking. Being grateful and not envious is a habit. Loving and not hating is a habit. Happiness is a habit."

J.C. let it all sink in for a few minutes and then said, "I want you to create your own daily mind routine after breakfast and start doing it every day."

CHAPTER THIRTY-TWO

THE VICTORY LOG

"Wealthy, successful people focus on their successes and not on their mistakes and failures, except to learn from them. They are success conscious. Anyone pursuing anything worthwhile in life, such as a goal, a dream, or their major purpose in life, will face seemingly insurmountable obstacles. They will make mistakes and they will face rejection and failure. All of the obstacles, mistakes, and failures are life's way of forcing individual evolution. Overcoming obstacles, mistakes, and failures forces you to a higher level. It improves your skill sets, knowledge, and focus. In short, it sharpens your knife.

A victory log is a list of all of your successes. Every time you realize any success, big or small, add it to your victory log. The victory log helps keep you success conscious and keeps you positive. When you are faced with obstacles that seem insurmountable, review your victory log. The victory log is your firewall that keeps doubts from entering your mind. It focuses your thinking on success and not on failure. Maintaining positive thinking is a key to success in life. Allowing doubts to enter your mind is negative thinking. Negative thinking prevents success from happening. It's water on your success fire."

When we got through our breakfast review, J.C. instructed me to create my own victory log and to keep adding to it during my life.

I looked over at Brendan. "The victory log I started with J.C. that summer has grown over the years. I keep it in the back of the notebook behind the *Rich Habits* book."

Brendan pulled it out and started going through it. There were over fifty pages. When he was done, he put it away and looked over to me.

"That's a lot of victories, Dad. You've been doing this since that summer?"

"Yep," I said. "That victory log is one of the reasons I keep the notebook by my side. I never know when I have to add something to the list. Any success, big or small, goes on that victory log."

"What's the next lesson?" I asked Brendan.

"Let's see. It's called the future mirror strategies," Brendan said.

"That's a good one," I responded. "They're a lot of fun. Really gets your imagination going crazy."

I then went on to explain J.C.'s future mirror strategies as he explained them to me.

CHAPTER THIRTY-THREE

THE FUTURE MIRROR STRATEGIES

"We touched on this a bit yesterday. There are four future mirror strategies:

1. **Ten-Year Future Letter**

2. **Five-Year Future Letter**

3. **One-Year Future Letter**

4. **Your Obituary**

TEN-YEAR FUTURE LETTER

The ten-year future letter you write to yourself describes how you have fulfilled all of your goals and dreams and realized your chief aim in life. It includes how much money you make, the house you live in, where you live, what car you drive, what you do for a living, how your family life has changed for the better, all of your real estate holdings, all of your investments, the amazing places you've traveled to, and how happy you are in your new life. Describe, in detail, what a typical day is like in your new future life from the minute you wake up to the minute you go to bed. The sky is the limit. Let your imagination run wild. Spare no details.

FIVE-YEAR AND ONE-YEAR FUTURE LETTERS

The five-year letter and one-year letter include all of your accomplishments made during each time period. Each letter lists all of the goals you accomplished during each time period. Each letter paints a picture of how your life has changed during each time period. Describe in each letter where you are financially, where you are mentally, how your job has changed for the better, how your family life has changed for the better, and what great things have happened during each time period.

OBITUARY

Write your own obituary. Your obituary describes the amazing life you've had. Like the letters, it describes all of the incredible things that have happened in your life that made you the super successful person that you were. Your obituary will share the great things you accomplished in life and how many lives you helped make better. It is the story of your amazing, incredibly successful life.

These strategies are your life plan. They map out your future life. They will help define the future you. They will help you define your goals and bring clarity to how you will accomplish each goal. They activate your subconscious mind to attract all of the things you want into your life. Your subconscious will then go to work, behind the scenes, to figure out how to accomplish your goals and realize your dreams and your chief aim in life. These strategies act like a magnet for success, drawing into your life all of the resources, skills, and relationships that will help you become the future you."

After breakfast, J.C. instructed me to take as much time as I needed to write my future letters and obituary. Afterward, he said, he had something special planned for us in the afternoon.

CHAPTER THIRTY-FOUR

CONQUERING FEAR

When I finished my future letters and obituary I headed over to J.C.'s office.

"Got 'em done," I said, raising my homework in the air. "Do you want to read them?" I asked.

"They're not for me. They're for you. They are all yours, my man," J.C. smiled through his words. "That's your life script you're holding in your hands. Your personal plans for your life. Those letters and that obituary are going to take you straight up. Like a rocket ship. Let's go."

That was all J.C. said, and we headed for the car.

"We're we going, J.C.?"

J.C. loved surprises. No matter how hard I tried, I couldn't get him to let me in on his secret plans for the afternoon.

We pulled into a large open field with a dozen hot air balloons bouncing up and down like anxious bobble heads.

"We're going up there." J.C. pointed straight up, into the sky.

The adrenaline immediately started to flood throughout my entire body.

"That one's ours." J.C. hoisted me up and into the carriage below this mountainous hot air balloon. The guide pulled on a cord and slowly we began to rise.

"So many people fear," J.C. said. "They fear life when they should be embracing it. Never fear. Fear holds you back. It stops you dead in its tracks. Those future letters and that obituary will take you places you never dreamed possible. There will be times when fear rears its head and tells you to pull back. Ignore it. That's just negative programming from your childhood. Don't let fear hold you back from your dreams."

As the balloon continued its ascent, I was growing anxious and moved away from the side of the carriage. I did my best not to look down. I didn't want J.C. to know I was afraid of heights. We weren't a hundred feet off the ground when the balloon suddenly stopped and started to drift under the control of the guide.

"Baby steps," J.C.'s voice boomed. "That's the only way to overcome fear. Take baby steps. If you're afraid of tackling something, do something small. Remember when your dad taught you to ride your bike?"

J.C. sensed my anxiety and was trying to distract me with another one of his stories.

"Well, you were scared. I remember. I was there. You had to be, whether you remember or not. You were wetting your pants. So what did your dad do? He took you and the bike on the grass in the backyard and for an hour you went back and forth, fifty feet at a time, falling, getting back on the bike, falling, getting back on the bike. When you had ten good runs, that's when your dad moved you to the driveway. After that we all piled into the station wagon and we spent another hour watching you ride your bike along the path. Baby steps."

J.C. lifted his head and looked at the sky.

"Conquering fear is about leaning in just a little until you build up enough confidence. Then you take it to the next level, whatever that is. You overcome fear by climbing the ladder one rung at a time.

"Look over there," J.C. said as he pointed his finger at one of the dozen balloons that were passing us by, one by one towards the heavens. J.C. moved to the edge of the carriage and nodded for me to follow him. J.C. was looking straight down.

"It's only a hundred feet," he said pleadingly.

I shuffled slowly towards the edge and grabbed the sides of the carriage tightly with both hands and leaned my head, ever so slightly, over the side to look down.

"I know you're afraid of heights," J.C. confided.

That's when I realized, for the first time, that the helicopter ride, the observation deck, the Statue of Liberty, and this balloon ride were part of J.C.'s master plan to help me conquer my greatest fear, heights.

"You need to make a habit out of conquering your fears. You begin by conquering your worst fears. That gives you the confidence to conquer all others."

I kept looking down. After a few minutes I could feel my grip begin to loosen. J.C. gave the guide a slight nod and, almost imperceptibly, we began to rise, very slowly. My grip loosened some more and soon my hands were resting on the side of the carriage. I turned towards J.C. and he could see from my grin that my fear was gone.

J.C. then called over to the guide, "How high can this thing go?"

The guide took us higher and higher, past all of the other balloons until they looked like little specks in the distance.

CHAPTER THIRTY-FIVE

THE RIDE BACK HOME

"You're so quiet." Mom had just picked me up from J.C.'s. We were headed back home. It was the most incredible summer of my life. I was sad it was over. I'd be back in school next week, and all I could think about was wanting to start the summer over with J.C. I wasn't in the mood to talk. I kept replaying all the lessons, the off weeks, the D.C. trip, and the balloon ride in my head, like a movie.

"So, did you have fun with J.C.?" Mom asked.

"Best summer ever," I said in a voice that gave away my mood.

"He's something, huh?" Mom was like a dentist, trying to pull the words out from my mouth.

"How was the balloon ride yesterday?"

I was surprised that she knew about our balloon ride. I realized, then, that J.C. must have been giving my parents daily updates during the summer. I remember feeling a sense of awe that my parents and J.C. would go to so much trouble just for me. That awe turned into a warm feeling that I realize now was love and gratitude. I look back on that summer and feel so lucky and so blessed to have had such a caring mentoring family.

"Amazing, Mom. It was so amazing. This was the best summer I've ever had. Thanks for making me do this. Sorry I gave you such a hard time about it."

My mom gave me a big kiss. "We all love you so much. That's what parents are supposed to do. We're supposed to do what's best for our kids, even if they don't like it or understand it. If we don't, who will? When the girls are older they'll spend a summer with J.C. too."

I looked over to my mom. "They're gonna love it."

I then turned to the backseat of the car, reached into my backpack, and pulled out the notebook. I learned so much from J.C. that summer. If I wasn't in awe of him before the summer, I was now. What an amazing guy, I thought to myself. I felt different. I knew my life would never be the same. J.C.'s lessons were now deep into my bones, woven together with intense emotions. They were a part of me now, forever. I was going to keep that notebook by my side forever.

Brendan closed the notebook. Silence enveloped the car. We were just pulling into South Bend and I decided to break the silence.

"There's the hall of fame." I pointed to the left, at the College Football Hall of Fame building. More silence. Brendan was lost in thought, absorbed by J.C. and my notebook.

Notre Dame was a blast. The campus was one big shrine. We visited the golden dome, took pictures in front of Touchdown Jesus, and watched Notre Dame squeak out a win. It was a magical experience, one neither of us would forget. And then it was over, and soon we were in our car for the long ride back to New Jersey.

"If I follow J.C.'s lessons, do you think it will help me get my grades up so I can get into Notre Dame?" Brendan asked.

"If you follow J.C.'s lessons," I responded, "you could get into Princeton, Bren. You could go anywhere you want."

Brendan reached into the backseat and retrieved my notebook, pulled out my copy of *Rich Habits*, and began reading. For the next three hours Brendan read the book cover to cover.

"Can I keep your *Rich Habits* book, Dad?" Brendan asked shortly after setting the book down on his lap.

"Sure, Bren. I've got a few spares around the house somewhere," I responded.

"Can I borrow your notebook, too?" Brendan already knew the answer.

"Sure. I'll make a copy of it for you. We'll put it in a binder so you can add to it," I smiled back.

"Cool," Brendan said.

Brendan spent much of the ride home reading through my notebook and reliving my summer with J.C. Then he took a nap. When he woke, we were on Route 78 in New Jersey, about an hour from home. We stopped to get a bite to eat and then got back in the car to finish our trip home.

"I'm gonna get into Notre Dame, Dad," Brendan said with an air of conviction.

"You are?" I replied.

"Yep. Gonna get into Notre Dame." Brendan turned his head and looked out the window and I thought I heard him murmur one more time, "Gonna get into Notre Dame."

Brendan graduated at the top of his class in high school. He made the National Honor Society in his junior year, not an easy achievement at his school. He was accepted to Notre Dame on early admission. When the acceptance letter arrived we were all ecstatic, so happy. I wished J.C. were alive to see it. To see how his rich habits, his teachings, and that notebook were transforming Brendan's life. I knew Brendan was on another path now. Another life forever changed by the famous J. C. Jobs. I felt content in knowing I had gone above and beyond my job as a parent. Thanks to J.C. and his lessons, I had become a success mentor to my son. I was proud. And I was happy.

ABOUT THE AUTHOR

Tom Corley understands the difference between being rich and poor: at age nine, his family went from being multi-millionaires to broke in just one night.

For five years, Tom observed and documented the daily activities of 233 wealthy people and 128 people living in poverty. He discovered there is an immense difference between the habits of the wealthy and the poor. During his research he identified over 200 daily activities that separated the "haves" from the "have nots." The culmination of his research can be found in his #1 bestselling book, *Rich Habits: The Daily Success Habits of Wealthy Individuals* (www.RichHabits.net).

Tom is a CPA, CFP and holds a master's degree in Taxation. He is also president of Cerefice and Company, CPAs, one of the top financial firms in New Jersey.

Tom has shared his insights on various network and cable television programs, such as *CBS Evening News*, Larry Kane's *Voice of Reason*, *Yahoo Financially Fit*, *The Dawn Show (Comcast – Philadephia)*, and many others. Nationally syndicated radio shows, such as *The Dave Ramsey Show*, *Marketplace Money*, and *WABC* (Laura Smith), have had Tom share his research with their listeners. He has also been featured in numerous print and internet publications, such as *Success Magazine*, *CNN*, *MSN Money*, *Kiplinger's Magazine*, and the *Huffington Post*.

International media attention for Corley and *Rich Habits* has resulted in publicity in Asia, the South Pacific, Europe, the United Kingdom, the Caribbean, and South America.

INDEX